This is Egypt...
Famous Egyptians

دي مصر...
مصريين مشهورين

lingualism

ISBN: 978-1-962752-15-2

Written by Ahmad Al-Masri and Matthew Aldrich

Edited by Hend Khaled and Matthew Aldrich

Audio by Heba Ali

website: www.lingualism.com

email: contact@lingualism.com

TABLE OF CONTENTS

INTRODUCTION

This book is the first in the (forthcoming) series دي مصر (This is Egypt...). Book One, **مصريين مشهورين** (Famous Egyptians) presents **twelve units**, each focusing on a significant figure who has shaped, or continues to shape, Egypt's cultural, political, or social life.

The texts are written entirely in Egyptian Arabic at an **advanced level (C1–C2)**, making them suitable for learners who have studied Lingualism's intermediate-level materials and are ready to push their language skills further. The writing style is clear yet sophisticated, offering learners an authentic challenge while staying accessible with support materials.

Each of the twelve units is built around a central text and is accompanied by:

- **Pre-reading questions** to activate background knowledge and spark curiosity

- **Key vocabulary** drawn from the text to support comprehension

- **Comprehension questions** to check understanding of details and main ideas

- **Discussion and essay prompts** to encourage critical thinking and deeper engagement

- **Professional audio recordings** of each text read by a native speaker from Cairo, to support listening practice and reinforce natural pronunciation and rhythm

Together, these features make the book not only a reading resource but also a complete toolkit for learners aiming to achieve a high level of proficiency in Egyptian Arabic.

HOW TO USE THIS BOOK

This book is designed to help you get the most out of your studies as you advance into the highest levels of Egyptian Arabic. To benefit fully, it's important to approach each unit actively and strategically. The following guide explains the steps you can take to make the most of the materials provided.

Unit Introductions and Pre-Reading Questions

Each unit begins with a short introduction in English. This introduction gives you some background about the person featured in the text. Having this context before you begin reading in Arabic helps activate your prior knowledge, set expectations, and make it easier to make educated guesses as you encounter new vocabulary and expressions.

The **Pre-Reading Questions** are designed to get you thinking about the subject. Try answering them in Egyptian Arabic, either by speaking out loud or writing your answers. If you are studying with a tutor or in a class, these questions can spark discussion. If you are studying on your own, they are still valuable to prepare your mind to notice key concepts and vocabulary when you read the text.

Vocabulary Exercise

Each unit highlights **10 Key Vocabulary items** from the text. These are words or phrases you will see in bold within the text (or underlined in a section title). Before reading, you are given their definitions in Arabic—but without the actual words themselves.

Your task is to match each definition to the correct word or phrase from the text. This activity forces you to pay close attention to both the definitions and the surrounding context in the text itself. Use clues from the sentences to help you decide which word matches which definition.

If you are studying with a teacher, you can work together to discuss possible matches before checking the answers. If you are studying alone, try to complete the activity on your own first, then check your answers using the **answer key** at the back of the book.

Approaching the Reading Text

The main text of each unit is a challenging article written in Egyptian Arabic. There is no tashkeel (vowel markings), just as you would see in authentic native materials. This means you must rely on your vocabulary knowledge, grammar skills, and context to determine the correct pronunciation and meaning.

There are many ways you can approach the text. Experiment with different methods to see what works best for you:

- **Listening First**: Play the audio without looking at the text. See how much you can understand by ear alone. Then listen again after studying the text to measure your progress.

- **Reading While Listening**: Follow along in the text while the narrator reads at a natural, native speed. Don't pause—just let yourself absorb as much as you can.

- **Reading Alone**: Read the text without audio, at your own pace. Focus on meaning, guess unknown words from context, and mark phrases you find difficult.

- **Checking with Audio**: Listen again while reading, and this time mark tashkeel only on words you were unsure of. Use the audio as a tool to confirm or correct your guesses.

The English translations are included at the back of the book—not beside the Arabic text. This is intentional. At this level, you should try to understand the text without relying too quickly on translations. Use them only when you are truly stuck.

Using the Audio

The recordings are available as a **free download from our website** and also to **stream on our YouTube channel**. The narrator speaks at a natural, conversational speed—faster than the recordings in our intermediate materials.

This is meant to challenge your listening comprehension at an advanced level. That said, if needed, you can slow down playback on YouTube. You can also repeat short sections of the audio to practice shadowing—reading the text out loud while trying to match the speaker's pronunciation, intonation, and rhythm.

Visit www.lingualism.com/audio, where you can find the free accompanying audio to download or stream (at variable playback rates).

Comprehension Questions

After the text, you will find **10 comprehension questions**. These test your understanding of the details, main ideas, and implications in the text. Try to answer them in Egyptian Arabic if you can.

- **On your own**: Write your answers in a notebook. Check back in the text to confirm, but avoid relying too much on the translation.

- **With a tutor or class**: Discuss your answers aloud. Let the questions guide you back into the text to justify your ideas.

Discussion and Essay Prompts

Finally, each unit includes open-ended questions designed for deeper reflection and critical thinking. These questions are not about right or wrong answers; they are meant to help you **express your opinions and ideas in Arabic**.

If you are studying independently, treat them as writing prompts. Write short essays or journal entries in Egyptian Arabic. If you are studying with a tutor, use them as conversation starters. They are especially useful for building fluency and practicing expressing complex ideas naturally.

Final Tip

There is no single "correct" path through a unit. Some learners prefer to listen first, then read. Others read first, then listen. The important thing is to challenge yourself, stay engaged, and use the different components—text, audio, vocabulary, and questions—in ways that push you beyond your comfort zone while still being manageable.

Above all, enjoy the journey. As you read about these remarkable Egyptians, you are not only improving your Arabic but also gaining insight into the history, culture, and voices that shape Egypt today. By the time you complete this book, you will not only have strengthened your command of Egyptian Arabic, but also prepared yourself to approach the wider series with confidence, curiosity, and a deeper connection to the language.

Bonus Materials: Podcast

Alongside the core content of this book, we are pleased to offer **free bonus materials** for extra listening practice. These are experimental resources created using **AI** to generate podcasts in Egyptian Arabic, each one based on the articles in this book.

In each podcast, two "speakers" discuss the themes and vocabulary of the unit's text in a conversational style. This makes the podcasts a great way to **review and consolidate** what you've learned by hearing familiar words and ideas used in a more natural, interactive setting.

The podcasts are available **only on our YouTube channel** (in the playlist for this book). To keep this strictly a listening activity, no Arabic transcripts are provided. Instead, you'll find **English translations** at the back of the book for support if needed.

While the podcasts sound very authentic, please note that they are **AI-generated** and occasionally contain minor imperfections. For example, you may notice an unusual pronunciation of certain letters, such as ق being pronounced /q/ instead of the common Egyptian /ʔ/, or ث as /th/ instead of /s/ in certain words. On very rare occasions, there may even be small grammar slips. However, each podcast has been carefully **reviewed and approved by a native Egyptian Arabic speaker**, and we believe these resources are not only reliable but also **highly valuable for learners**, precisely because they add a layer of variety and realism.

نجيب محفوظ

Naguib Mahfouz is widely regarded as one of the greatest writers in modern Arabic literature. His novels capture the spirit of Egyptian society, from the bustling streets of Cairo to the personal struggles of ordinary people. Known for his clear, powerful storytelling, Mahfouz explored themes like family, tradition, and change in a way that speaks to readers of all generations. His works have been translated into many languages, earning him international recognition and making him a bridge between Egyptian culture and the world. Even today, his stories remain a window into the heart of Egypt.

Pre-Reading Questions

1. تعرف كاتب مصري أو عربي بتحبه؟ ليه؟ بتحب أيه في أسلوبه أو المواضيع اللي بيكتب عنها؟

2. هل فيه كتب أو روايات أثّرت على طريقتك في التفكير؟ إزاي؟

3. لما تسمع اسم "نجيب محفوظ"، بتفتكر أيه؟ سمعت عنه قبل كده؟ قريتله حاجة؟

Vocabulary

Below are ten definitions. Each one matches a word or phrase that appears in bold in the reading text (or underlined in a section title).

Before reading, try to understand each definition and think of what Arabic term might fit.

Then, as you read, look for the bold words and phrases in the text. Use the surrounding context to help you match them to the definitions.

An answer key is provided at the back of the book.

١. الحكومة تاخد ممتلكات حد من غير موافقته، غالباً لأسباب سياسية أو قانونية

٢. الناس اللي مش أغنيا جداً ولا فُقرا جداً، دخلهم متوسط

٣. جمع قهوة، أماكن الناس بتقعد فيها، تشرب شاي أو قهوة، وتتكلّم

٤. حاجة كبيرة اتسابِت من شخص بعد وفاته، زي أفكاره أو شغله

٥. شخص بيكتب عن التغيرات اللي بتحصل في المجتمع وأسلوب الناس في الحياة

٦. شديد، بيحب النظام والانظباط ومابيقبلش أي تهاون

٧. شكله بسيط لكن في الحقيقة فيه عمق وصعوبة مخفية

٨. عنده شغف أو رغبة قوية من جواه تجاه حاجة معينة

٩. فهمه وإدراكه للحاجات اللي حواليه

١٠. مواجهة أو خلاف مباشر بين شخصين أو أفكار

نجيب محفوظ: حكايات من قلب الحارة

نجيب محفوظ هو واحد من أشهر الكُتّاب اللي مصر أنجبتهم في القرن العشرين. ناس كتير بتقول إنه مش بس كاتب، ده مؤرخ اجتماعي وثقافي لمصر. كتب عن الناس، عن الشوارع، عن الحارات، عن القهاوي، عن الأحلام والآلام. واللي يقراله يحس إنه ماشي في شوارع القاهرة القديمة بنفسه.

الطفولة والبداية

نجيب محفوظ اتولد في حيّ الجمالية، في قلب القاهرة، سنةْ ١٩١١. الحي ده كان مليان حياة: صوت البيّاعين في الشوارع، ريحة الأكل من البيوت، صوت الأذان والأطفال اللي يلعبوا في الحارات. الحياة دي أثّرت في وَعْيه من طفولته، وفضلت معاه طول عمره، وده باين جداً في كتاباته.

كان أصغر واحد في إخواته، وده خلّاه يعيش جزء كبير من طفولته لوحده في البيت. فبقى بيقضي وقت طويل في القراية. كان بيحب يقرا كل حاجة: قصص، كتب دينية، تاريخ، وأدب أوروبيّ كمان. من هنا، بدأت تتكوّن شخصيته ككاتب.

لما خلص المدرسة، دخل كلية الآداب، قسم فلسفة، في جامعة القاهرة. وده كان قرار مش تقليدي في الوقت ده. بس نجيب كان جواه حب حقيقي للفكر والتأمّل.

من الفلسفة للأدب

بعد ما اتخرج، اشتغل موظف في الحكومة، وفضل يتنقّل من وزارة لوزارة. ورغم إن الشغل كان بياخد وقت، لكنه كان دايماً بيلاقي وقت للكتابة. في الأول، كتب قصص قصيرة، وبعد كده بدأ يكتب روايات طويلة.

في بداياته، كان متأثر بالتاريخ الفرعوني، وكتب روايات زي "كفاح طيبة" و"عبث الأقدار". لكن بعد كده، بدأ يسيب التاريخ ويركز على الواقع، على الناس اللي

حواليه، على الطبقة المتوسطة والفقيرة، على القاهرة اللي بتتغير يوم بعد يوم.

الثلاثية والتحوّل الكبير

أشهر أعماله هي "الثلاثية": "بين القصرين"، "قصر الشوق"، و"السكرية". الروايات دي بتحكي قصة عيلة مصرية عادية، من وقت الاحتلال البريطاني لحد بعد ثورة ١٩٥٢. الشخصيات فيها واقعية جداً، فيها الأب الصارم، والأم الطيبة، والأولاد اللي كل واحد فيهم ماشي في طريق مختلف.

الثلاثية دي مش بس روايات عن عيلة، دي مراية لمصر كلها في الفترة دي. وده اللي خلى ناس كتير تعتبرها من أعظم الأعمال الأدبية في العالم العربي.

أسلوبه في الكتابة

أسلوب نجيب محفوظ سهل ممتنع. الجمل بسيطة، بس فيها عمق. الشخصيات دايماً بتتكلم زي الناس العاديين، بس أفكارهم فيها فلسفة، فيها تساؤلات عن الحياة، والموت، والحرية، والدين، والحب.

كمان نجيب كان عنده قدرة غريبة على تصوير الأماكن. يعني لما تقراله، تحس بريحة الشارع، تسمع صوت العربيات، وتشوف ألوان البيوت. كان بيخلي القارئ يعيش جو الرواية مش بس يقراها.

السياسة والرقابة

رغم إن نجيب محفوظ ما كانش ناشط سياسي، لكنه كتب عن قضايا سياسية واجتماعية مهمة. في رواياته، هتلاقي نقد للفساد، والاستبداد، والتعصّب. وعشان كده، أعماله أحياناً كانت بتتصادر أو تتمنع.

رواية "أولاد حارتنا" مثلاً، اتعرضت لهجوم كبير، واتهموه بالإساءة للدين، رغم

إنه قال أكتر من مرة إنه ما كانش يقصد كده. الهجوم ده وصل لدرجة إن شخص حاول يقتله في التسعينات وطعنه في رقبته.

ورغم كده، نجيب محفوظ ما كانش بيحب يتخانق أو يدخل في جدال. كان دايماً هادي، مؤمن بحرية الفكر، بس من غير صدام.

نوبل والتكريم العالمي

في سنة ١٩٨٨، فاز نجيب محفوظ بجايزة نوبل في الأدب. وده كان حدث تاريخي، لأنه أول كاتب عربي ياخد الجايزة دي. العالم كله بدأ يتكلم عنه، وأعماله اترجمت للغات كتير.

لكن نجيب كان بسيط، ما حبّش الشهرة. وفضل قاعد في نفس البيت، وبيروح نفس القهوة، ويكلم نفس أصحابه.

نهاية هادية وميراث ضخم

في آخر سنين عمره، صحته بقت ضعيفة، خصوصاً بعد محاولة اغتياله. بقى صعب عليه يكتب بإيده، فكان بيملي القصص على واحد من أصحابه. وفضل يكتب لحد آخر أيامه.

مات نجيب محفوظ سنة ٢٠٠٦، عن عمر ٩٤ سنة. بس هو لسه عايش في قلوب الناس، وفي صفحات كتبه اللي بتتباع لحد النهاردة.

هو مش بس كاتب، هو سجل حيّ لمصر في القرن العشرين. وعشان كده، كل واحد عايز يفهم مصر، لازم يقرأ لنجيب محفوظ.

Comprehension Questions

1. نجيب محفوظ اتولد فين؟ وإزاي المكان ده أثّر على كتاباته؟

2. ليه كان بيقضي وقت طويل لوحده في طفولته؟ وإزاي استغل الوقت ده؟

3. درس أيه في الجامعة؟ وليه كان اختياره غير تقليدي؟

4. أيه المواضيع اللي كتب عنها في بداية حياته الأدبية؟

5. "الثلاثية" بتحكي عن أيه؟ وليه الناس شايفينها مهمة؟

6. أيه مواصفات أسلوب نجيب محفوظ في الكتابة؟ اذكر صفة واحدة وشرحها.

7. نجيب محفوظ كتب عن السياسة؟ إزاي؟

8. أيه اللي حصل بعد ما نشر رواية "أولاد حارتنا"؟

9. إمتى فاز بجايزة نوبل؟ وكان أيه رد فعله؟

10. بعد وفاته، أيه اللي بيفضل من ميراث نجيب محفوظ الأدبي في رأيك؟

Discussion / Essay Prompts

1. هل شايف إن الأدب فعلاً ممكن يعكس حياة المجتمع؟ ادّي أمثلة من روايات أو أفلام أو كُتّاب تانيين.

2. لو قابلت نجيب محفوظ النهاردة، تحب تسأله عن أيه؟ وليه؟

3. في رأيك، أيه أهمية إن كاتب ياخد جايزة زي نوبل؟ بتغيّر حاجة فعلاً؟

يسرا

Yousra has been one of the most beloved and enduring figures in Egyptian and Arab entertainment for over four decades. With a wide range of roles across film and television, she has built a career marked by versatility, elegance, and emotional honesty. Audiences connect with her not only for her talent on screen, but for the warmth and grace she brings to everything she does. Her presence remains strong across generations, making her a lasting symbol of artistic excellence and cultural influence.

Pre-Reading Questions

1. في رأيك، أيه اللي بيخلي الفنان/ة يفضل محبوب لفترة طويلة؟

2. هل الجمال كفاية علشان ينجح الممثلة؟ ليه أو ليه لأ؟

3. هل بتشوف إن الفنان له دور اجتماعي أو إنساني؟ ولا بس دوره بيقتصر على التمثيل؟

Vocabulary

Read the definitions below. Each one matches a bold word or phrase in the text. Try to guess the terms first, then find them in context as you read. Answers are at the back of the book.

1. أجيال مختلفة متتابعة عبر الزمن

2. تخلّي الناس دايماً يشوفوها بشكل محترم ومتّزن

3. تعاون بين اتنين، خصوصاً في التمثيل أو الغِنا

4. تعبّر عن إحساس الشخصية بشكل يوصل للجمهور

5. تفاهم وتناغم بين شخصين بيخلّيهم يشتغلوا كويس سوا

6. تلمس مشاعرهم أو تخلّيهم يتأثروا

7. توصل لطموحاتها وتثبت وجودها

8. شخص أو عمل فني الناس بتفتكره عبر الزمن

9. شخصية عامة بتمثل قضايا إنسانية في الأمم المتحدة

10. شخصية مشهورة ومحبوبة جداً، بتمثل الفن بشكل مميز وملهم

يسرا: وشوش كتير... بس قلب واحد

يسرا فنانة ليها مكانة مميزة في قلوب المصريين والعرب. موهبتها، حضورها، وشخصيتها الراقية خلّوها تفضل من أهم نجمات الفن لأكتر من أربعين سنة. قدرت توازن بين أدوار متنوعة ومسيرة مستقرة، وقدّمت فن بيقرب من الناس وبيعبر عنهم بصدق.

البدايات

اسمها الحقيقي سيفين حافظ نسيم، اتولدت سنة ١٩٥٥، وبدأت مشوارها الفني في أواخر السبعينات. في البداية، اشتغلت في أدوار صغيرة في السينما، بس بسرعة الناس ابتدت تاخد بالها من حضورها المتميز، وابتدت تلفت الأنظار.

رغم إنها كانت جميلة جداً، لكن ما اعتمدتش بس على شكلها. كانت بتشتغل على نفسها، وبتحاول تطوّر أداءها، وتختار أدوار تبين موهبتها الحقيقية.

انطلاقتها الحقيقية

في التمانينات، بدأت يسرا تتعاون مع المخرج الكبير يوسف شاهين، وده كان نقلة مهمة في مشوارها. شاركت معاه في أفلام زي حدوتة مصرية، وإسكندرية كمان وكمان، وده عرّف الجمهور على يسرا بشكل جديد: ممثلة مثقفة، عميقة، ومختلفة.

كمان كان ليها تعاون طويل مع النجم عادل إمام، وكونوا سوا ثُنائي ناجح في أفلام كتير، منها الإنس والجن، كراكون في الشارع، الإرهاب والكباب، وغيرها. الناس كانت بتحب تشوفهم سوا، لأن فيه بينهم كيميا حقيقية على الشاشة.

التليفزيون ودخولها البيوت المصرية

يسرا ما اكتفتش بالسينما، لكن كمان نجحت جداً في التليفزيون. مسلسلاتها دايماً كانت بتمسّ الناس، وبتدخل بيوتهم بكل ترحيب.

من أشهر مسلسلاتها:

- أين قلبي
- قضية رأي عام
- لحظات حرجة
- خيانة عهد
- حرب أهلية

أدوار يسرا دايماً كانت متنوعة: أم، زوجة، قاضية، دكتورة، أو ست بتواجه تحديات الحياة. دايماً بتعرف توصل مشاعر الشخصية للناس بطريقة بسيطة وحقيقية.

يسرا الإنسانة

بعيد عن التمثيل، يسرا معروفة برقتها وتواضعها. بتشارك في مبادرات خيرية كتير، وبتدعم قضايا زي حقوق المرأة، ومكافحة السرطان، والتعليم.

كمان هي سفيرة نوايا حسنة للأمم المتحدة، وبتشارك في فعاليات ثقافية وإنسانية في مصر والعالم العربي. بتستخدم شهرتها عشان تساعد، مش بس عشان تظهر كنجمة كبيرة.

رمز للمرأة العصرية

يسرا بالنسبه لناس كتير مش بس ممثلة، هي نموذج للمرأة القوية، الناجحة، اللي قدرت تحقّق نفسها وتحافظ على احترام الناس. عمرها ما كانت طرف في

فضيحة، دايماً محافظة على صورتها، ودايماً بتتكلم بحكمة واتزان.

لبسها، كلامها، اختياراتها... كلها بتعكس ذوق راقي ووعي. وبكده، بقت أيقونة في الفن، والموضة، والحياة الاجتماعية.

يسرا في عيون الجيل الجديد

رغم إنها بقالها سنين طويلة في المجال، إلا إن يسرا لسه ليها جمهور كبير من الشباب. بتعرف تجدد نفسها، وتشتغل مع مخرجين وممثلين جداد، وبتوصل لأجيال مختلفة.

ظهورها في المسلسلات الرمضانية بقى من الحاجات اللي الناس بتستنّاها كل سنة، ودايماً عندها حاجة جديدة تقولها، سواء في التمثيل أو في المواقف العامة.

من الشاشة لقلوب الجمهور

على مدار مشوارها، فضلت يسرا محافظة على حضورها الخاص، وبقت جزء من الذاكرة الفنية في مصر والعالم العربي. جيل ورا جيل، بيحبها ويتابعها، لأنها عارفة توصل للناس ببساطة، وتفضل دايماً قريبة من قلوبهم.

Comprehension Questions

1. أيه اسم يسرا الحقيقي، وبدأت مشوارها الفني إمتى؟

2. أيه الدور اللي لعبه يوسف شاهين في مشوارها؟

3. إزاي تعاونها مع عادل إمام أثّر على شهرتها؟

4. اذكر ٣ من أشهر مسلسلاتها، وأيه اللي بيخلّي الناس تحب أدوارها؟

5. أيه الجوانب الإنسانية في شخصية يسرا؟

6. ليه الناس بتشوف يسرا نموذج للمرأة العصرية؟

7. إزاي بتتواصل يسرا مع الجيل الجديد؟

8. في رأيك، أيه اللي خلى يسرا تفضل ناجحة لأكتر من ٤٠ سنة؟

9. هل شهرتها أثرت على سلوكها العام؟ وضّح.

10. إزاي قدرت يسرا توازن بين حياتها الفنية والإنسانية؟

Discussion / Essay Prompts

1. هل بتتفق إن الفنان الناجح لازم يكون عنده دور مجتمعي؟ ناقش.

2. الشهرة بتخلي الفنان أقرب أو أبعد عن الناس؟ اشرح برأيك.

3. مين فنان/ة مصري/ة شايف إنه/ها بيمثل/بتمثل نموذج محترم وقدوة؟ وليه؟

رفاعة الطهطاوي

Rifa'a al-Tahtawi played a key role in laying the foundations of Egypt's modern intellectual and educational life. As a scholar, translator, and reformer in the 19th century, he helped introduce new ideas while staying rooted in Egyptian and Islamic identity. His vision centered on education, progress, and cultural exchange, offering a model of renewal based on understanding rather than imitation. His influence continues to shape conversations about knowledge, reform, and national development.

Pre-Reading Questions

1. هل تعتقد إن التعليم هو المفتاح الرئيسي لتقدم أي بلد؟ ليه أو ليه لأ؟

2. في رأيك، هل ممكن الاستفادة من الحضارات التانية من غير ما نضيّع هويتنا؟

3. أيه أهمية الترجمة في نقل العلوم والمعرفة بين الشعوب؟

Read the definitions below. Each one matches a bold word or phrase in the text. Try to guess the terms first, then find them in context as you read. Answers are at the back of the book.

1. أفكار أو قيم أساسية الناس بتمشي عليها في حياتها أو شغلها

2. اتباع حاجة من غير تفكير أو نقد

3. المحافظة على الهوية مع تطوير الفكر

4. تطور شامل في العلم والفكر والمجتمع

5. شخص الناس بتعتبره نموذج ومصدر تشجيع

6. شعور مفاجئ بالاختلاف الكبير بين ثقافتين

7. لحظة أو حدث بيغيّر مجرى حياة الشخص أو مصيره

8. مجموعة بيسافروا يتعلموا برة البلد علشان يرجعوا ينقلوا اللي اتعلموه

9. مكان لتعليم اللغات والترجمة

10. يشرح الأفكار بطريقة سهلة وواضحة

رفاعة الطهطاوي: بداية مصر الحديثة

رفاعة الطهطاوي كان له دور كبير في تشكيل مصر الحديثة في القرن الـ ١٩. كان عالم ومترجم ومجدد، واشتغل علشان يفتح باب لتفكير جديد. من خلال جهوده في نشر العلوم الحديثة، وتطوير التعليم، والتقريب بين الثقافات، ساهم في بناء أساس للتقدم يربط بين الأصالة والتجديد.

من الصعيد للأزهر

اتولد رفاعة سنة ١٨٠١ في مدينة طهطا في الصعيد. من صغره كان بيحب القراية والتعلُّم، وأهله شجعوه يروح الأزهر في القاهرة. هناك، درس الفقه، اللغة، والتفسير، وكان من أنبه الطلبة.

في الأزهر، اتأثر بكذا شيخ منفتح، وكان بيفكّر بطريقة مختلفة شوية عن باقي الطلبة. ما كانش بيكتفي بالحفظ، كان دايماً بيسأل ويحاول يفهم المعاني الأعمق.

رحلته لفرنسا: صدمة حضارية

سنة ١٨٢٦ وهو لسه شاب، تم اختياره يسافر فرنسا مع أول بعثة تعليمية أرسلها محمد علي باشا. في الأول، راح كـ إمام ديني للمجموعة، لكن مع الوقت، بدأ يتعلم اللغة الفرنسية، ويتعمق في الثقافة الأوروبية.

قعد هناك حوالي خمس سنين. درس فيها الفلسفة، السياسة، الهندسة، والعلوم الحديثة. كل حاجة شافها هناك كانت جديدة بالنسباله: طريقة التعليم، احترام القانون، دور المرأة، واهتمام الناس بالعلم.

الرحلة دي كانت نقطة تحوّل في حياته، وخلّته يرجع مصر وهو شايف الدنيا بشكل مختلف تماماً.

نقل المعرفة مش بس الترجمة

لما رجع مصر، بدأ يشتغل في الترجمة، بس ما كانش مجرد بيحوّل كلام من لغة للغة، هو كان بينقل أفكار، مبادئ، ونظرة جديدة للعالم.

اشتغل في مدرسة الطب، ومدرسة الألسن، وساهم في ترجمة كتب من مجالات متعددة: تاريخ، جغرافيا، علوم، وسياسة. كان دايماً بيحاول يبسّط المفاهيم علشان الناس تفهمها، ويختار المصطلحات بعناية علشان تكون قريبة من العقل المصري.

التعليم في قلب مشروعه

رفاعة كان مؤمن إن النهضة مش هتحصل من غير تعليم. علشان كده، اشتغل بقوة على تطوير المناهج، وإنشاء مدارس جديدة، مش بس للأولاد، لكن كمان للبنات. كان شايف إن تعليم البنات مش تهديد، بالعكس، هو أساس لتقدم المجتمع كله.

اهتم كمان بتدريب المُدرسين، وتنظيم المدارس، وكتب كتب تعليمية بالعربي كانت جديدة على الناس وقتها.

مشروع ثقافي كبير

بعيداً عن التعليم، رفاعة كان عنده مشروع ثقافي أوسع. كان بيحاول يخلق نوع من التوازن: نستفيد من الحضارة الغربية، من غير ما نقلدها تقليد أعمى، ونحتفظ في نفس الوقت بجذورنا الإسلامية والعربية.

ما كانش بيشوف تعارض بين الدين والعلم، ولا بين الأصالة والتجديد. كان دايماً بيحاول يفتح باب للحوار، ويقنع الناس بالتطور عن طريق الفهم مش الصدام.

مصاعب ومواقف سياسية

رغم إن شغله كان علمي وثقافي، لكن ما قدرش يبعد عن السياسة. اشتغل في أكتر من منصب رسمي، وكان قريب من صُنّاع القرار. بس أحيانا كانت أفكاره مش مقبولة من بعض الجهات، وده خلاه يتعرض للضغوط، وتم نقله أو إبعاده أكتر من مرة.

لكن حتى في أصعب الفترات، فضل متمسك بمبادئه، ومكمل في شغله، سواء في التعليم أو الترجمة أو الكتابة.

أثره اللي لسه مستمر

اتوفى رفاعة الطهطاوي سنة ١٨٧٣ لكن تأثيره لسه باقي لحد النهاردة. كتير من المدارس اللي اتبنت بعده كانت ماشية على نفس خطه. وكتير من المثقفين شافوه قدوة ومُلهم، سواء في القرن الـ ١٩ أو بعد كده.

أفكاره عن التعليم، دور المرأة، العلاقة بين الدين والعلم، وقيمة الترجمة، بقت جزء من النقاش الثقافي في مصر والعالم العربي.

أول خطوة في طريق طويل

اللي عمله رفاعة ما كانش ثورة كاملة، لكنه كان أول خطوة في طريق التغيير. فتح أبواب جديدة، وخلّى ناس كتير تبدأ تفكر بشكل مختلف.

فضل طول عمره مؤمن إن العلم والتربية هما الأساس، وإن الشعب المصري يستحق تعليم يخلّيه ينهض، ويكون في مستوى أفضل بلاد العالم.

Comprehension Questions

1. رفاعة الطهطاوي اتولد فين؟ ودرس فين؟

2. إزاي أثرت عليه رحلته لفرنسا؟

3. أيه الفرق بين ترجمته للكتب وبين الترجمة التقليدية؟

4. ليه كان شايف إن تعليم البنات مهم؟

5. أيه اللي كان بيميز مشروعه الثقافي؟

6. هل شغله كان بعيد عن السياسة؟ وضّح.

7. أيه اللي اتعرضله بسبب أفكاره؟

8. إزاي فضل مؤثر حتى بعد وفاته؟

9. ناقش الجملة: "ما كانش ثورة كاملة، لكن كانت أول خطوة في طريق التغيير"

10. أيه العلاقة اللي شافها بين الدين والعلم في رأيه؟

Discussion / Essay Prompts

1. في رأيك، أيه أهم التحديات اللي بتواجه أي حد بيحاول إصلاح في بلده؟

2. هل شايف إن أفكار رفاعة الطهطاوي لسه مناسبة لوقتنا؟ ليه؟

3. ناقش فكرة "الاستفادة من الغرب من غير تقليد أعمى". إزاي ممكن يحصل توازن فعلاً؟

جمال عبد الناصر

Gamal Abdel Nasser was a powerful force in shaping modern Egypt and the wider Arab world. As a revolutionary leader and later president, he inspired millions with his vision of national dignity, social justice, and Arab unity. His speeches, bold decisions, and deep connection with the people left a lasting impact on generations. Whether admired or debated, his legacy continues to echo in conversations about leadership, independence, and the meaning of true change.

Pre-Reading Questions

1. في رأيك، أيه صفات القائد السياسي الناجح؟ وهل لازم يكون دايماً محبوب؟

2. سمعت قبل كده عن جمال عبد الناصر؟ أيه اللي تعرفه عنه أو عن ثورة ٢٣ يوليو؟

3. يعني أيه "كرامة وطنية" بالنسبالك؟ وهل شايف إن دي حاجة الناس لسه بيدوروا عليها النهاردة؟

Vocabulary

Read the definitions below. Each one matches a bold word or phrase in the text. Try to guess the terms first, then find them in context as you read. Answers are at the back of the book.

١. إحساس الشعب بالفخر والانتماء وعدم قبول الإهانة أو الاحتلال

٢. إن الدولة تستولي على ملك خاص وتخليه تابع للحكومة

٣. استحمل وفضل واقف قدام الصعوبات أو الأعداء

٤. الاسم اللي بيتقال على الهزيمة في حرب يونيو ١٩٦٧

٥. الهجوم اللي حصل على مصر من بريطانيا وفرنسا وإسرائيل سنة ١٩٥٦

٦. سلسلة من المعارك بين مصر وإسرائيل بعد النكسة لتحضير الجيش المصري

٧. فكرة إن العرب يكونوا أمة واحدة موحدة سياسياً واقتصادياً

٨. كلام مهم أوي قاله زعيم أو سياسي في لحظة مؤثرة في التاريخ

٩. مجموعة الظباط المصريين اللي عملوا ثورة ٢٣ يوليو ١٩٥٢

١٠. يسيب منصب أو سلطة بشكل رسمي

.

جمال عبد الناصر: قائد الثورة وصوت الكرامة

جمال عبد الناصر هو واحد من أكتر الشخصيات اللي أثّرت في تاريخ مصر الحديث. اتولد في وقت كانت فيه مصر لسه تحت تأثير الاحتلال البريطاني، وكبر وهو شايف الظلم، والفقر، وعدم المساواة. الحاجات دي كلها كانت بداية لمشوار طويل من التغيير والصراع من أجل الكرامة الوطنية.

النشأة وبداية الوعي

اتولد عبد الناصر سنة ١٩١٨ في حي باكوس في الإسكندرية، بس أصله من محافظة بني سويف. أبوه كان موظف بسيط في البريد، واتنقل كتير بين المحافظات، وده خلى جمال يعيش في أكتر من مكان في طفولته.

من وهو طفل، كان مهتم بالسياسة. شارك في مظاهرات ضد الاحتلال، وكان بيقرا جرايد وكتب عن الاستقلال والثورات. دخل الكلية الحربية سنة ١٩٣٧، وهناك اتعرّف على ظباط تانيين بيشاركوه نفس الأفكار، وابتدوا يحلموا بتغيير حقيقي في البلد.

ثورة ٢٣ يوليو ١٩٥٢

بعد سنين من الفساد، واتساع الفجوة بين الأغنيا والفقرا، وهيمنة الاحتلال البريطاني، قرر عبد الناصر مع مجموعة من الظباط (اللي اتسمّوا بعد كده "الظباط الأحرار") إنهم يخططوا لانقلاب عسكري. وفعلاً، في ليلة ٢٣ يوليو ١٩٥٢، سيطروا على مواقع حساسة في القاهرة، وأجبروا الملك فاروق على التنازل عن العرش.

في البداية، كان محمد نجيب هو رئيس مجلس قيادة الثورة، لكن بعد صراعات داخلية، أصبح عبد الناصر هو القائد الحقيقي، وفي سنة ١٩٥٦، انتُخب رسمياً رئيساً لمصر.

تأميم قناة السويس

من أهم اللحظات في تاريخ عبد الناصر، كانت في ٢٦ يوليو ١٩٥٦، لما أعلن في خطاب تاريخي إنه قرر يأمم قناة السويس. القرار ده جه بعد ما أمريكا وبريطانيا رفضوا يموّلوا مشروع السد العالي، فقرر يستخدم دخل القناة علشان يموّل المشروع بنفسه.

ردّ الفعل ما كانش سهل. شنّت بريطانيا وفرنسا وإسرائيل هجوم عسكري على مصر في أكتوبر ١٩٥٦، اللي اتعرف بعد كده باسم "العدوان الثلاثي". لكن الشعب المصري صمد، والدعم الدولي لمصر، خصوصاً من أمريكا والاتحاد السوفيتي، وقف، وانسحبت القوات المعتدية.

التأميم كان ضربة كبيرة للاستعمار، وخلّى عبد الناصر بطل قومي مش بس في مصر، لكن في العالم العربي كله.

الوحدة العربية والحلم القومي

عبد الناصر كان عنده حلم بوحدة العرب، وإن الشعوب العربية تكون كتلة واحدة قوية. في ١٩٥٨، حصل اتحاد بين مصر وسوريا تحت اسم "الجمهورية العربية المتحدة"، لكن الاتحاد ده ما استمرش غير ٣ سنين.

رغم فشل الاتحاد، إلا إن فكرة القومية العربية فضلت حية. عبد الناصر كان شايف إن تحرير فلسطين، والتخلص من الاستعمار، وبناء اقتصاد عربي مشترك، هي أهداف لازم العرب كلهم يتحدوا لتحقيقها. كانت خطاباته دايماً قوية ومؤثرة، وكان بيكلم الناس بلغة بسيطة، قريبة من القلب، وده خلّى الملايين يحبوه ويتأثروا بيه.

النكسة والصمود

في يونيو ١٩٦٧، حصلت نكسة كبيرة لما إسرائيل هجمت على مصر وسوريا والأردن، واحتلت سينا والضفة الغربية والجولان. كانت الهزيمة صدمة كبيرة، وناس كتير وجهت اللوم لعبد الناصر.

في يوم ٩ يونيو، طلع عبد الناصر في خطاب وقال إنه قرر يتنحى عن الحكم. بس في اليوم اللي بعده، نزل ملايين المصريين الشارع يهتفوا إنه لازم يكمّل. قدام طوفان الحب ده، قرر يرجع عن التنحي.

ورغم الهزيمة، إلا إن عبد الناصر بدأ يعيد بناء الجيش، وبدأت مصر في حرب الاستنزاف، استعداداً لمعركة تحرير سينا.

الوفاة والميراث

في ٢٨ سبتمبر ١٩٧٠، فجأة، مات جمال عبد الناصر بأزمة قلبية، وكان عمره ٥٢ سنة بس. خبر وفاته صدم الوطن العربي كله، وحضر جنازته الملايين في القاهرة.

رغم إن آراء الناس عن عبد الناصر بتختلف، لكن محدّش يقدر ينكر إنه غيّر وجه مصر، وخلّى الكرامة الوطنية والعدالة الاجتماعية تبقى مطالب مشروعة.

الناس لحد النهاردة لسه بتسمع خطاباته، ولسه بتفتكر مواقفه، ولسه بتحكي عن "زمن عبد الناصر".

Comprehension Questions

1. عبد الناصر اتولد فين؟ وإزاي أثرت نشأته في تفكيره؟

2. أيه اللي خلى الظباط الأحرار يعملوا انقلاب سنة ١٩٥٢؟

3. ليه عبد الناصر قرر يأمم قناة السويس؟

4. أيه اللي حصل بعد التأميم؟ وإزاي مصر واجهت العدوان الثلاثي؟

5. أيه الهدف من الجمهورية العربية المتحدة؟ وليه ما استمرتش؟

6. أيه نوع اللغة اللي كان بيستخدمها عبد الناصر في خطاباته؟

7. أيه اللي حصل في نكسة ١٩٦٧؟ وكان أيه رد فعل عبد الناصر؟

8. الناس عملت أيه بعد إعلان عبد الناصر التنحي؟

9. عبد الناصر بدأ يعمل أيه بعد الهزيمة؟

10. إزاي الناس بتفتكره لحد النهاردة؟ وبتقول أيه عن "زمن عبد الناصر"؟

Discussion / Essay Prompts

1. هل شايف إن الكاريزما أو طريقة الكلام عند الزعيم بتأثر في حب الناس ليه؟ إدّي مثال من عبد الناصر أو حد تاني.

2. هل فشل الوحدة العربية معناه إن الحلم القومي انتهى؟ ولا لسه ليه معنى لحد النهاردة؟

3. لو كنت عايش وقت نكسة ٦٧، كنت هتحس بأيه؟ وهل كنت هتأيد قرار عبد الناصر بالتنحي؟

رانيا المشاط

Rania Al-Mashat is a leading figure in Egypt's economic and political landscape. With a strong academic background and international experience, she has taken on major roles in government and global institutions. Her work reflects a clear vision, modern communication style, and dedication to sustainable development. Al-Mashat represents a new generation of leadership in Egypt—confident, capable, and deeply engaged with the challenges of today's world.

Pre-Reading Questions

1. في رأيك، هل لازم الوزير يكون عنده خلفية أكاديمية قوية؟ ليه؟

2. إزاي ممكن تكون المرأة عنصر فعال في السياسة والاقتصاد؟

3. هل وجود مسؤول نشيط على السوشيال ميديا بيساعد في بناء ثقة الناس؟ وضّح.

Vocabulary

Read the definitions below. Each one matches a bold word or phrase in the text. Try to guess the terms first, then find them in context as you read. Answers are at the back of the book.

1. إن كل حاجة تبقى واضحة ومفهومة، من غير ما يكون فيه إخفاء أو غموض

2. خطط لتحسين وضع الاقتصاد في البلد

3. شخصية واضحة بتلفت الانتباه

4. شكل أو أسلوب حديث ومتطور

5. قرارات البنك المركزي اللي بتأثر على الفلوس في السوق

6. مؤسسة عالمية بتساعد الدول في الأزمات الاقتصادية

7. مشروعات بتفيد المجتمع على المدى الطويل

8. مناقشة بين أطراف مختلفة علشان يوصلوا لاتفاق أو يحلّوا مشكلة

9. منظمات كبيرة بتشتغل بين الدول، زي البنك الدولي وصندوق النقد الدولي

10. نظام بيسهّل الشغل بين جهات مختلفة

رانيا المشاط: اقتصاد، دبلوماسية، وتمكين

رانيا المشاط من الوجوه اللي ظهرت بقوة في الحياة السياسية والاقتصادية في مصر في السنين الأخيرة. ست عندها حضور، ثقة بالنفس، وطريقة كلام بتجمع بين الجدية واللباقة. قدرت توصل لمناصب كبيرة، وتكون مثال للبنت المصرية المتعلمة والطموحة، اللي بتقدر تمثّل بلدها في أكبر المحافل الدولية.

البدايات والتعليم

اتولدت رانيا سنة ١٩٧٥، ونشأت في بيت بيهتم بالتعليم. من وهي صغيرة كانت بتحب الأرقام، التحليل، والأسئلة الكبيرة عن الاقتصاد والمجتمع. درست الاقتصاد في الجامعة الأمريكية في القاهرة، وهناك كانت دايماً من الأوائل.

بعد التخرج، كملت دراستها في أمريكا، وخدت ماجستير ودكتوراه في الاقتصاد من جامعة ميريلاند. دراستها كانت مركّزة على الاقتصاد الكلي، السياسات النقدية، والأسواق العالمية.

البنك المركزي المصري وصندوق النقد الدولي

رجعت رانيا مصر واشتغلت في البنك المركزي المصري في قسم السياسات النقدية. وهناك، اشتغلت على تطوير أدوات جديدة، وشاركت في تحديث السياسة الاقتصادية.

بعد كده، اشتغلت في صندوق النقد الدولي (IMF) في واشنطن، وكانت واحدة من أصغر المصريين اللي وصلوا لموقع مستشار اقتصادي هناك. شاركت في مفاوضات مع دُوَل كتير، وسافرت بلاد مختلفة عشان تساعد في وضع برامج إصلاح اقتصادي.

السنين دي كانت مهمة جداً في تشكيل شخصيتها كمحللة، وخبرتها زادت في التعامل مع الأزمات والتفاوض مع الحكومات.

وزيرة السياحة في وقت صعب

في ٢٠١٨، تم تعيينها وزيرة للسياحة في مصر. كانت فترة صعبة جداً، لأن السياحة كانت لسه ما رجعتش لقوتها بعد أحداث ٢٠١١.

اشتغلت رانيا المشاط بطريقة مختلفة. ركّزت على التسويق لمصر بصورة عصرية، وبدأت حملة اسمها "People to People" علشان توري العالم جمال الناس في مصر مش بس الأماكن الأثرية. كمان أطلقت حملة " Experience Egypt" اللي بتستخدم السوشيال ميديا بشكل حديث علشان توصّل صورة إيجابية للعالم.

اشتغلت على تدريب العاملين في قطاع السياحة، واهتمت بتحسين جودة الخدمات. وده بدأ يساعد على رجوع السياحة واحدة واحدة.

وزارة التعاون الدولي

في ٢٠٢٠، تم تعيينها وزيرة للتعاون الدولي. وده منصب بيحتاج توازن كبير بين الدبلوماسية، الاقتصاد، والتفاوض. مهمتها كانت تنسيق العلاقات مع المؤسسات الدولية، زي البنك الدولي، الاتحاد الأوروبي، والوكالات التنموية.

رانيا بتشتغل على ربط التمويل بالتنمية المستدامة. يعني مش بس ناخد قروض، لكن نستخدمها في مشاريع تنفع الناس: مدارس، مستشفيات، طاقة متجددة، وبنية تحتية.

أطلقت رانيا "منصة التعاون التنسيقي المشترك" عشان تسهّل التعاون بين الحكومة والشركاء الدوليين. ودايماً كانت بتركّز على الشفافية والتواصل، وبتنشر تقارير علنية عن كل المشاريع والمبالغ اللي بتمولها.

تمثيل مصر دولياً

مثّلت رانيا مصر في مؤتمرات كتير حوالين العالم، من الأمم المتحدة للمنتدى الاقتصادي العالمي في دافوس. بتتكلم إنجليزي بطلاقة، وبتعرف تشرح مواقف مصر بطريقة منظمة ومقنعة.

ناس كتير في الإعلام الغربي اعتبروها وجه حديث لمصر، وبيشوفوا فيها نموذج للمرأة القادرة على قيادة ملفات معقدة بثقة وكفاءة.

أسلوبها وتواصلها

الناس لاحظت أسلوبها المختلف: لبس أنيق، لغة واضحة، وأسلوب منظم في الكلام. دايماً بتتكلم بأرقام، وبتحب الشفافية، وبترد على الأسئلة بطريقة مباشرة.

هي كمان نشيطة على السوشيال ميديا، خصوصاً إكس (اللي كان اسمه تويتر)، وبتستخدم المنصة دي عشان تعرض شغلها، وتشرح إنجازات الوزارة، وتشارك صور من الزيارات والاجتماعات.

قيادية بروح عصرية

رانيا المشاط لسه في عز نشاطها، لكن تأثيرها واضح. قدرت تغيّر صورة المرأة في المناصب الوزارية، وقدّمت نموذج للقيادة اللي بتعتمد على العلم والخبرة.

بنات كتير بيشوفوها مصدر إلهام، وناس كتير شايفين إن مصر محتاجة أكتر من نوع القيادات دي: منظمة، شفافة، وبتشتغل على المدى الطويل.

Comprehension Questions

1. أيه اللي كان بيميز رانيا المشاط في طريقتها وأسلوبها؟

2. أيه الدراسات اللي عملتها برا مصر؟ وإزاي أثرت على شغلها؟

3. إزاي طورت قطاع السياحة لما كانت وزيرة؟

4. أيه الفرق بين شغلها في وزارة السياحة ووزارة التعاون الدولي؟

5. أيه اللي كانت بتحاول توصله من خلال "منصة التعاون التنسيقي المشترك"؟

6. إزاي رانيا بتستخدم السوشيال ميديا في شغلها؟

7. ليه الإعلام العالمي بيعتبر رانيا المشاط وجه حديث لمصر؟

8. إزاي كانت بتربط التمويل بالتنمية المستدامة؟

9. هل طريقة لبسها وطريقتها في التواصل كان ليهم تأثير على الناس؟ إزاي؟

10. في رأيك، أيه اللي خلى رانيا المشاط مصدر إلهام لبنات كتير؟

Discussion / Essay Prompts

1. هل بتعتقد إن المرأة في مصر دلوقتي عندها فرص حقيقية للقيادة؟ ناقش بمثال.

2. في رأيك، أيه أهمية الشفافية في شغل الوزارات؟ وهل رانيا المشاط نجحت في ده؟

3. إزاي ممكن نتأكد إن القروض الخارجية بتستخدم في مشاريع فعلاً بتفيد الناس؟

محمد صلاح

Mohamed Salah's journey from a small village in Egypt to the top of international soccer has made him more than just an athlete. He is a symbol of determination, humility, and what hard work can achieve. Loved not only for his talent but also for his character, Salah has become a role model for millions, especially young people who see their own dreams in his story. His impact goes far beyond the field, representing pride, hope, and possibility for Egypt and the Arab world.

Pre-Reading Questions

1. تعرف حد بدأ من بيئة بسيطة وحقق نجاح كبير؟ تحب تشارك القصة؟

2. في رأيك، أيه الصفات اللي بتميز لعيب الكورة الناجح؟ وهل الشهرة بتأثر على شخصية الإنسان؟

3. إزاي ممكن الرياضيين يكونوا قدوة إيجابية للشباب؟ وهل بتشوف إن ده دور مهم فعلاً؟

Vocabulary

Read the definitions below. Each one matches a bold word or phrase in the text. Try to guess the terms first, then find them in context as you read. Answers are at the back of the book.

1. ابتدى يبقى معروف ومشهور بسبب شطارته أو تميّزه

2. اهتمامه إنه يطوّر نفسه ويتدرّب ويتحسّن دايماً

3. تعبير معناه إن الرحلة كانت فيها تعب وصعوبات

4. تعبير معناه إن النجاح بييجي بعد تعب وشغل ومجهود

5. تغيير مهم في الحياة أو الشغل بيغيّر كل حاجة

6. شخص الناس بتشوف فيه أمل للمستقبل وتحقيق الأحلام

7. شخص الناس بتقلّده أو بتتعلم منه بسبب نجاحه أو أخلاقه

8. لسه فيه أهداف وأحلام جاية ولسه الرحلة ما خلصتش

9. موقف صعب محتاج مجهود كبير علشان تعدّيه

10. يورّي للناس إنه شاطر ويستاهل الفرصة

محمد صلاح: من قرية نجريج لقمة العالمية

محمد صلاح ماهواش بس نجم كورة؛ ده بقى رمز للأمل، والطموح، والتعب اللي بيؤدي للنجاح. كل طفل في مصر بقى يشوف فيه مثال حقيقي إن الحلم ممكن يتحقق، مهما كانت البداية بسيطة.

البداية من نجريج

اتولد محمد صلاح سنة ١٩٩٢ في قرية اسمها نجريج، في محافظة الغربية. قرية بسيطة، وبيت بسيط، وأسرة عادية. من وهو صغير، كان بيعشق الكورة. كان بيلعب في الشارع، في المدرسة، في أي حتة مفتوحة.

كان أهله دايماً واقفين جنبه، بس الطريق ما كانش سهل. عشان يروح التمرين في نادي المقاولين العرب في القاهرة، كان بيصحى بدري جداً، يركب أكتر من مواصلة، ويرجع آخر اليوم تعبان، لكنه ما اشتكاش.

الاحتراف في أوروبا

بعد ما لمع نجمه مع المقاولين، جاله عرض من نادي بازل السويسري سنة ٢٠١٢. السفر برة مصر كان تحدي كبير، خصوصاً إنه ما كانش يعرف اللغة، ولا العادات، ولا الأجواء. بس محمد صلاح كان عنده إصرار غريب، وكان مركز على هدفه: النجاح.

ومن بازل، انتقل لتشيلسي، بس ما خدش فرصته هناك. ناس كتير كانوا بيقولوا إنه مش هيكمل، لكنه قرر يثبت نفسه. راح إعارة لفورينتينا، وبعدين لروما، وهناك بدأت الناس تاخد بالها منه بجد.

وفي ٢٠١٧، حصلت النقلة الكبيرة، لما انضم لليفربول. ومن أول موسم، بقى نجم الفريق، وحقق أرقام قياسية، وفاز بجوايز كتير، منهم هدّاف الدوري الإنجليزي.

شغله على نفسه

اللي بيميز محمد صلاح مش بس موهبته، لكن شغله المستمر على نفسه. دايماً محافظ على لياقته، بيتمرن أكتر من المطلوب، بيهتم بأكله ونومه، وحتى حياته الشخصية بعيدة عن المشاكل.

هو شخص هادي، متواضع، دايماً مبتسم، وده خلى الناس تحبه مش بس في مصر، لكن في كل العالم. جمهوره في إنجلترا بيغنوله في المدرجات، وفي العالم العربي الأطفال بيعلّقوا صوره في أوضهم.

فخر لمصر والعرب

محمد صلاح مش بس لاعب كورة، هو بقى رمز لمصر. لما بيشارك مع منتخب مصر، بيكون الكل مستنيه. كان ليه دور كبير في تأهل مصر لكأس العالم ٢٠١٨، بعد غياب طويل. الناس كانت بتبكي من الفرحة، وصلاح كان في قلب اللحظة دي.

صلاح كمان دايماً بيرجع لقريته، وبيساعد أهلها، وبيتبرع لمستشفيات ومدارس ومساجد. عمره ما نسي أصله، وده خلى الناس تحترمه أكتر.

النجاح مش صدفة

قصة محمد صلاح بتعلمنا إن النجاح مش بييجي بالصدفة. هو تعب، وصبر، ووقع، وقام، وفضّل يحلم ويجري ورا حلمه. كان دايما بيقول إن الفشل مش النهاية، وإن كل يوم فرصة جديدة.

الشباب في مصر والعالم العربي بقوا يشوفوا فيه قدوة. مش بس في الكورة، لكن في الأخلاق، والطموح، والإصرار.

لسه المشوار مكمل

محمد صلاح لسه صغير، ولسه قدامه سنين كتير في الملاعب. بس حتى لو بطل كورة بكرة، تأثيره هيفضل. هو علّم جيل كامل إن ابن قرية صغيرة ممكن يلمع في أكبر الملاعب.

صلاح مش بس فخر مصر، هو فخر العرب، وفخر لأي حد بيؤمن إن الحلم ممكن يتحقق لو تعبت عشان توصلله.

Comprehension Questions

1. محمد صلاح اتولد فين؟ وكانت أيه ظروفه وهو صغير؟

2. إزاي كان بيروح التمرين؟ وأيه اللي ده بيقولهولنا عن شخصيته؟

3. فين كانت أول محطة احتراف لمحمد صلاح في أوروبا؟

4. ليه ما نجحش في تشيلسي؟ وإزاي واجه التحدي ده؟

5. إزاي كانت نقلة ليفربول مختلفة في مسيرته؟

6. أيه اللي بيخلّي محمد صلاح محبوب مش بس في مصر؟

7. إزاي بيهتم بصحته ولياقته؟

8. أيه الحاجات اللي بيعملها لصالح قريته وأهله؟

9. إزاي قصة صلاح بتلهم الشباب؟

10. ليه تأثير محمد صلاح ممكن يفضل حتى بعد ما يبطل كورة؟

Discussion / Essay Prompts

1. هل الشهرة ممكن تغيّر شخصية الإنسان؟ هل شايف إن محمد صلاح قدر يحافظ على تواضعه؟

2. في رأيك، أيه الحاجات المفيدة اللي ممكن الشباب يتعلموها في حياتهم؟

3. لو عندك حلم كبير، أيه الحاجات اللي ممكن تتعلمها من صلاح علشان توصله؟

أم كلثوم

No other artist has left a mark on Arabic music like Umm Kulthum. With a voice that moved audiences to tears and lyrics that blended love, longing, and pride, she became much more than a performer. For millions, her songs were a shared emotional experience, tying personal memories to national identity. Her monthly concerts were major cultural events, and her presence reached across borders and generations. To this day, Umm Kulthum remains a timeless symbol of musical artistry in the Arab world.

Pre-Reading Questions

1. تعرف فنان أو فنانة صوتهم بيأثر فيك؟ إزاي الصوت والموسيقى ممكن يغيّروا مشاعر الناس؟

2. أيه الأغاني أو المطربين القدام اللي بتحبهم؟ ليه بتحس إن الأغاني القديمة مختلفة؟

3. تعرف أيه عن أم كلثوم؟ سمعت صوتها قبل كده؟ عندك أغنية مفضّلة ليها؟

Vocabulary

Read the definitions below. Each one matches a bold word or phrase in the text. Try to guess the terms first, then find them in context as you read. Answers are at the back of the book.

١. أنيقة أو محترمة، فيها ذوق عالي

٢. إحساس قوي بالكلمات والمشاعر الجميلة اللي فيها فن

٣. اسم الهزيمة في حرب ١٩٦٧ بين مصر وإسرائيل

٤. الإحساس بالقيمة والاحترام، وعدم القبول بالإهانة

٥. جزء من الأغنية بيتكرر أكتر من مرة

٦. حب الشخص لبلده واستعداده يضحي علشانها

٧. رد فعل الناس وقت العرض، زي التسقيف أو الهتاف

٨. لحظة أو إحساس إن حد بيمشي أو بيبعد عنك

٩. موكب أو مراسم بعد وفاة شخص علشان الناس تودّعه

١٠. ناس بتحب تسمع الموسيقى أو الغُنا جدا، وبتفهم فيه

أم كلثوم: صوت مصر والعالم العربي

لو فيه صوت واحد بس نقدر نقول عليه "صوت مصر"، يبقى من غير تفكير: أم كلثوم. الست اللي اتربّت في قرية صغيرة، وبقت بعد كده أيقونة في الفن العربي، مش بس في مصر، لكن في كل البلاد اللي بتتكلم عربي. صوتها كان فيه قوة وإحساس، وكلام أغانيها كان فيه شاعرية، وطنية، وحب.

الطفولة والبدايات

أم كلثوم اتولدت سنة ١٩٠٤ تقريباً، في قرية صغيرة اسمها طماي الزهايرة، في محافظة الدقهلية. أبوها كان شيخ وبيعلم الأطفال القرآن، وهي كمان بدأت تحفظ القرآن من وهي صغيرة. ومن كتر ما كان صوتها قوي وواضح، أبوها ابتدى ياخدها تغنّي معاه في حفلات دينية وأفراح بسيطة.

في الأول، الناس ما كانوش يعرفوا إنها بنت، لأنها كانت بتلبس لبس ولاد وهي بتغنّي، عشان المجتمع ما كانش فكرة إن بنت تطلع تغنّي قدام الناس. بس مع الوقت، صوتها كان بيخلي الكل ينسى الشكل، ويسمع بالقلب.

من الريف للقاهرة

لما كبرت شوية، بدأ صيتها يوصل القاهرة. واحد من الناس اللي سمعوا عنها كان الشيخ أبو العلا محمد، وهو اللي شجّعها تسيب القرية وتيجي القاهرة. وكانت خطوة كبيرة جداً في حياتها.

في القاهرة، اتعرّفت على شعراء وملحنين كبار، زي أحمد رامي، محمد القصبجي، زكريا أحمد، وبعدين رياض السنباطي. كل واحد فيهم ساهم في إنها تطور نفسها أكتر وأكتر، وتبقى "كوكب الشرق" زي ما الناس سمتها بعدين.

الشهرة والجمهور

في التلاتينات والأربعينات، أم كلثوم بقت نجمة كبيرة. حفلاتها كانت بتتذاع في الراديو، والقهاوي كانت بتتملي بالسمّيعة. الناس كانوا بيستنّوا أول خميس من كل شهر عشان يسمعوا حفلتها الجديدة.

اللي يميّز حفلاتها إنها كانت ساعات تغنّي نفس الكوبليه أكتر من مرة بسبب تفاعل الجمهور. لو الجمهور قال "الله!"، كانت تعيد الجملة بصوت أقوى أو بشكل مختلف. العلاقة بين أم كلثوم والجمهور كانت مش طبيعية، فيها حب متبادل وفهم عميق.

أغانيها واللغة

كلام أغاني أم كلثوم كان دايماً فيه بلاغة وشاعرية. كتير من الأغاني كتبها أحمد رامي، اللي كتب لها أكتر من ١٠٠ أغنية. كلمات الأغاني كانت بتتكلم عن الحب، الفراق، الكرامة، وحتى السياسة.

ومن أشهر أغانيها:

- "إنت عمري"
- "الأطلال"
- "سيرة الحب"
- "فكروني"
- "أمل حياتي"
- "على باب مصر"
- "مصر تتحدث عن نفسها"

اللغة في أغانيها كانت فصحى أحياناً، وأحياناً عامية راقية. وده خلى ناس من كل المستويات الثقافية تقدر تستمتع بيها.

أم كلثوم والسياسة

أم كلثوم مكانتش بعيدة عن السياسة. أيام ثورة ١٩٥٢، وقفت مع الظباط الأحرار، وكانت أغانيها فيها دعم واضح للثورة. بعد كده، كانت علاقتها بالرئيس جمال عبد الناصر قوية، وكان هو كمان بيحب يسمعها جداً.

في فترة حرب ١٩٦٧، وبعد النكسة، بدأت أم كلثوم تعمل حفلات في بلاد عربية زي لبنان، تونس، والمغرب، وجمعت فلوس كتير علشان تساند الجيش المصري. كانت الناس شايفة إنها مش بس مطربة، لكن رمز للوطنية.

تأثيرها في العالم العربي

مفيش فنانة أثّرت في العرب زي أم كلثوم. في المغرب كانوا بيسموها "الست"، وفي العراق كانوا بيسمعوا حفلاتها وهما سهرانين بالليل، وفي لبنان كان جمهورها بيعيد أغانيها كلمة كلمة.

حتى بعد ما ماتت، لسه صوتها بيتذاع في الراديو، ولسه ناس جديدة بتكتشفها كل يوم. فيه ناس بيقولوا: "فيه مطربين كتير، بس مفيش غير أم كلثوم واحدة بس."

الوفاة والميراث

اتوفّت أم كلثوم سنة ١٩٧٥، وجنازتها كانت من أكبر الجنازات اللي شافتها مصر. ملايين من الناس نزلوا الشوارع يودّعوها. كانوا شايفين إنها مش بس فنانة، لكنها جزء من حياتهم، من ذكرياتهم، من هويتهم.

لحد النهاردة، أم كلثوم لسه موجودة. موجودة في الأغاني، في الصور، في الأفلام الوثائقية، وفي قلب كل واحد بيحب الغُنا الأصيل.

Comprehension Questions

1. أم كلثوم اتولدت فين وبدأت تغني إزاي؟

2. ليه كانت بتلبس لبس ولاد في بداياتها؟

3. مين ساعدها تروح القاهرة؟ وأيه اللي حصل لما راحت هناك؟

4. أيه دور أحمد رامي، القصبجي، والسنباطي في مشوارها؟

5. أيه اللي كان مميز في حفلات أم كلثوم؟

6. كانت أيه طبيعة العلاقة بين أم كلثوم والجمهور؟

7. أيه المواضيع اللي كانت بتغني عنها؟

8. أيه اللي بيربط أم كلثوم بالسياسة؟

9. كان أيه رد فعلها بعد النكسة؟ عملت أيه؟

10. إزاي لسه تأثير أم كلثوم باين في العالم العربي بعد وفاتها؟

Discussion / Essay Prompts

1. هل شايف إن الفن ممكن يكون له دور سياسي أو وطني؟ إدّي مثال من حياة أم كلثوم أو فنان تاني.

2. في رأيك، أيه اللي خلى أم كلثوم مختلفة عن باقي الفنانين؟ الصوت؟ الكلمات؟ العلاقة مع الجمهور؟

3. لو أم كلثوم كانت عايشة النهاردة، تفتكر كانت هتنجح بنفس الشكل؟ ليه أو ليه لأ؟

مجدي يعقوب

Magdi Yacoub is one of the world's most respected heart surgeons and a figure deeply admired in Egypt and beyond. His medical work has saved countless lives, and his dedication to helping others has inspired generations. After decades of groundbreaking surgery abroad, he returned to Egypt to expand access to life-saving care. Through both science and compassion, Yacoub has become a symbol of excellence, service, and human dignity.

Pre-Reading Questions

1. تفتكر إن العلم لوحده كفاية علشان يخلّي الإنسان ناجح؟ ولا لازم يكون فيه كمان قيم إنسانية؟

2. تعرف أطباء أو علماء مصريين مشهورين؟ أيه اللي بيميزهم؟

3. في رأيك، هل ممكن الشخص يعيش في الخارج بس يفضل مرتبط ببلده؟ ليه أو ليه لأ؟

Vocabulary

Read the definitions below. Each one matches a bold word or phrase in the text. Try to guess the terms first, then find them in context as you read. Answers are at the back of the book.

1. أخت أبوه

2. إنه شايف اللي بيعمله مسؤولية مش منّة

3. إنه ما يتكبرش رغم نجاحه

4. البُعد عن الوطن والناس والأهل

5. بيأثر تأثير كبير وباقي في الناس أو المكان

6. درس مجال معين بعمق، زي القلب أو العيون

7. شخص الناس بتحب تقلده أو تمشي على طريقه

8. طرق وأدوات طبية جديدة ومتطورة

9. علاج من غير ما المريض يدفع فلوس

10. عمل جراحات

مجدي يعقوب: طبيب القلوب ومحبوب الناس

في ناس بتدخل التاريخ علشان شهرتهم، وفي ناس بتدخله علشان أثرهم. مجدي يعقوب من النوع التاني. راجل مصري، طبيب قلب، لكنه مش بس دكتور ناجح... ده إنسان بيسيب بصمة في كل قلب بيعالجه، وكل شاب بيلهمه، وكل فقير بيساعده.

الطفولة والبداية

اتولد مجدي يعقوب سنة ١٩٣٥ في مدينة بلبيس بمحافظة الشرقية، في عيلة قبطية مثقفة. أبوه كان دكتور، وده كان له تأثير كبير عليه. من وهو صغير، كان بيتفرج على أبوه وهو بيكشف على المرضى، وبيشوف بعينيه قد أيه الطب ممكن يغيّر حياة الناس.

لكن اللحظة اللي غيّرت مصيره كانت لما عمته اتوفّت فجأة بسبب مشكلة في القلب. ساعتها قرر إنه يخصص حياته لدراسة جراحة القلب، عشان محدش تاني يفقد شخص بيحبّه بنفس الطريقة.

السفر والتعليم في إنجلترا

بعد ما خلّص مجدي يعقوب دراسته في كلية الطب في جامعة القاهرة، سافر إنجلترا عشان يتخصّص أكتر. هناك، واجه تحديات كتير: اللغة، الغُربة، وضغط الشغل. لكن كان عنده شغف، وإصرار، وموهبة مش طبيعية.

اشتغل في مستشفيات كبيرة، وكان دايماً بيحب يتعلّم الجديد، وبيجرب تقنيات حديثة. وبعد سنين من الشغل والتعب، بقى من أشهر جراحين القلب في العالم.

إنجازات عالمية

من أكبر إنجازاته إنه ساعد في تطوير تقنيات زراعة القلب، وكان بيجري عمليات معقدة جداً لمرضى كان الأمل عندهم شبه منعدم. في التمانينات، بقى رئيس قسم جراحة القلب في مستشفى "هيرفيلد" في لندن، وهناك أجرى أكبر عدد من عمليات زراعة القلب في أوروبا.

اتكرّم بجوايز كتير، أهمها إنه أخد لقب "سير" من الملكة إليزابيث سنة ١٩٩٢، وده أعلى وسام في بريطانيا. لكن هو كان دايماً بيقول إن أهم تكريم ليه هو ابتسامة مريض بعد ما يخفّ.

الرجوع لمصر والعمل الخيري

رغم إنه عاش أغلب عمره في إنجلترا، إلا إن مجدي يعقوب عمره ما نسي مصر. كان دايماً بيحلم إنه يرجع يخدم بلده. وفعلاً، في ٢٠٠٩، أسّس مركز مجدي يعقوب للقلب في أسوان، واللي بيوفر علاج مجاني تماماً لمرضى القلب، خصوصاً الأطفال.

المركز ده بقى من أفضل الأماكن في الشرق الأوسط في جراحة القلب، وبيستقبل آلاف المرضى من مصر والدول العربية. كمان فيه تدريب للأطباء والممرضين، وأبحاث علمية متطورة.

تواضع وإنسانية

رغم كل النجاح، فضل مجدي يعقوب معروف بتواضعه الشديد. مش بيحب يتكلم عن نفسه، ودايماً شايف إن اللي بيعمله "واجب مش فضل". بيقضي ساعات طويلة في العمليات، وبيتواصل مع المرضى بعين الأب، مش بس الدكتور.

هو مؤمن إن العلم لازم يخدم الناس، وإن الطب من غير رحمة ملوش معنى.

وعشان كده، هو مش بس طبيب، لكنه كمان قدوة وإنسان نادر.

مشوار مابين العلم والإنسانية

النهاردة، مجدي يعقوب بقى رمز مش بس للنجاح العلمي، لكن كمان للخير والعطاء. شباب كتير في مصر والعالم العربي بيشوفوه مثل أعلى، وبيقولوا إنهم عايزين يبقوا زيه.

هو مثال حيّ إنك ممكن توصل للعالمية، وتفضل وفي لجذورك، وتستخدم علمك في خدمة الناس.

Comprehension Questions

1. مجدي يعقوب اتولد فين، وأيه اللي خلاه يختار مجال جراحة القلب؟

2. أيه التحديات اللي قابلها لما سافر إنجلترا؟

3. أيه أهم إنجازاته في مجال جراحة القلب؟

4. ليه مركز القلب في أسوان يعتبر حاجة مهمة جداً؟

5. إزاي بيجسد مجدي يعقوب معنى التواضع في حياته؟

6. هل كان هدفه الشهرة ولا حاجة تانية؟

7. اتكلم عن علاقته بمصر رغم إنه عاش في إنجلترا؟

8. إزاي بيساعد شباب الأطباء؟

9. أيه سبب اختيار مجدي يعقوب لتخصص جراحة القلب؟

10. إزاي ساهم مركز أسوان للقلب في خدمة المجتمع المصري والعربي؟

Discussion / Essay Prompts

1. هل شايف إن كل شخص ناجح لازم يرد الجميل للمجتمع؟ ناقش.

2. إزاي ممكن نزرع في الشباب حب خدمة الناس؟

3. لو كنت دكتور/ة، تحب تتخصص في أيه وليه؟ وهل إنت شايف في مجدي يعقوب مصدر إلهام؟

عمر الشريف

Omar Sharif rose to international fame as one of Egypt's most recognized film actors. His roles in both Egyptian and global cinema made him a familiar face across cultures. He began his career in Cairo before taking on major roles in Hollywood, where he earned critical acclaim and global attention. Despite his years abroad, his name remained closely tied to Egyptian identity and pride. His story reflects a life shaped by ambition, talent, and the pull between two worlds.

Pre-Reading Questions

1. هل تعرف ممثل مصري أو عربي وصل للسينما العالمية؟ أيه الصعوبات اللي ممكن تقابل فنان في المشوار ده؟

2. في رأيك، هل الشهرة العالمية تستاهل التضحيات الشخصية؟ ليه؟

3. أيه الفرق بين التمثيل في السينما المصرية والسينما الأجنبية من وجهة نظرك؟

Vocabulary

Read the definitions below. Each one matches a bold word or phrase in the text. Try to guess the terms first, then find them in context as you read. Answers are at the back of the book.

١. تعبير عن شخص أو شيء بيربط بين ثقافتين مختلفتين

٢. حياته خدت اتجاه جديد ومختلف تماماً

٣. حياته ما كانتش سهلة وكان فيها قرارات صعبة

٤. رحّب بيه وقدّمله فرص كبيرة

٥. شخص الناس بتفتكره على إنه كان بيمثّل عصر كامل

٦. عمل حاجات مهمة لدرجة إنها لسه مؤثرة بعده

٧. قصة حب مشهورة وكان الكل بيتكلم عنها

٨. مشاعر متضاربة جواه مش عارف يحلّها

٩. ناس كتير في العالم يعرفوه ويتابعوه

١٠. يمثّل أقل من قبل كده، من غير ما يوقف تماماً

عمر الشريف: نجم من مصر إلى هوليوود

عمر الشريف مش بس ممثل مشهور، ده كان جسر بين الشرق والغرب، بين مصر والعالم. من أول ما ظهر على الشاشة، والناس حست إنه مختلف. شكله، حضوره، طريقته في الكلام... كل ده خلاه نجم بسرعة. لكن اللي خلى عمر الشريف يفضل في الذاكرة مش بس شكله أو موهبته، لكن كمان رحلته اللي كانت مليانة تحديات واختيارات صعبة.

طفولته وبداياته في مصر

اتولد عمر الشريف سنة ١٩٣٢ في إسكندرية، في عيلة مسيحية كاثوليكية من أصل لبناني. اسمه الحقيقي كان ميشيل شلهوب. من وهو صغير، كان بيحب التمثيل، وكان بيمثل في المسرحيات المدرسية. بعد كده دخل الجامعة الأمريكية في القاهرة، ودرس الرياضيات والفيزياء، لكن قلبه كان مع الفن.

أول خطوة حقيقية في مشواره كانت لما قابله المخرج يوسف شاهين، واختاره علشان يمثل في فيلم صراع في الوادي سنة ١٩٥٤، قدام فاتن حمامة، اللي بعد كده بقت مراته.

حب حياته: فاتن حمامة

قصة حب عمر الشريف وفاتن حمامة كانت حديث الناس. رغم إنهم كانوا من ديانتين مختلفين، عمر غيّر ديانته علشان يتجوزها. كانوا بيشكلوا ثنائي فني ناجح جداً، وشاركوا في أكتر من فيلم.

لكن بعد سنين، بسبب سفر عمر للخارج وانشغاله في السينما العالمية، حصل انفصال بينهم. ورغم كده، كان دايماً يقول إن فاتن كانت حب حياته الحقيقي، وإنه ما حبش غيرها.

الطريق لهوليوود

في أوائل الستينات، جاله عرض يمثل في فيلم لورانس العرب (Lawrence of Arabia)، وده كان انطلاقة كبيرة له على مستوى العالم. دوره في الفيلم ده عمله شهرة ضخمة، واترشح لجايزة الأوسكار، وكسب جولدن جلوب.

بعد كده، شارك في أفلام عالمية تانية، زي Doctor Zhivago، وFunny Girl مع باربرا سترايسند، واللي اتقال إن كان بينهم قصة حب.

لكن رغم النجاح، كان عمر الشريف دايماً حاسس بالغربة. ما كانش مرتاح أوي في حياة هوليوود، وكان أوقات كتير بيشتاق لحياته في مصر.

الهوية والانتماء

رغم شهرته العالمية، لكن عمر الشريف عمره ما نسي مصر. كان دايماً يتكلم عن بلده بحب، وكان حاسس إنه "ابن النيل" حتى وهو عايش في باريس أو لوس أنجلوس. لكنه في نفس الوقت كان حاسس إنه ما ينفعش يرجع لمصر بسهولة، خصوصاً بعد الانفصال عن فاتن، وبعد ما اتغيّرت حياته تماماً.

حياته كانت مليانة صراعات داخلية: بين حب الشهرة، والشعور بالوحدة. بين الغرب اللي فتح له أبوابه، والشرق اللي اشتاق له.

السنين الأخيرة والوفاة

في آخر سنين حياته، قلّل عمر الشريف من التمثيل، وبدأ يعيش حياة هادية. في ٢٠١٥، اتوفى بسبب أزمة قلبية، بعد ما كان بيعاني من الزهايمر في آخر أيامه.

لما مات، مصر كلها حزنت عليه. مش بس لأنه نجم عالمي، لكن لأنه كان رمز لجيل كامل، لجيل كان بيحلم، وبيحب السينما، وبيشوف في عمر الشريف صورة لنجاح مصري وصل للعالمية.

ميراثه الفني

عمر الشريف ساب وراه تاريخ طويل من الأفلام المهمة، سواء في مصر أو برة. ساب صورة الراجل الشرقي الجذاب في أذهان الناس، وخلّى اسم مصر يتقال في أكبر مهرجانات السينما.

هو مش بس فنان، هو قصة نجاح، وقصة حب، وقصة صراع مع النفس. وعشان كده، عمر الشريف هيفضل في الذاكرة، مش بس كممثل، لكن كرمز لجسر بين حضارتين.

Comprehension Questions

1. عمر الشريف اتولد فين؟ وكان أيه اسمه الحقيقي؟

2. إزاي بدأت علاقته بالتمثيل؟ ومين اللي اكتشفه؟

3. ليه غير ديانته؟ وأيه اللي حصل بعدين في علاقته بفاتن حمامة؟

4. أيه الدور اللي خلاه يتشهر عالمياً؟

5. أيه نوع الأدوار اللي مثّلها في هوليوود؟ ونجح فيها إزاي؟

6. هل عمر الشريف كان مرتاح في حياة الشهرة؟ وضّح ليه أو ليه لأ

7. إزاي كان بيشوف مصر وهو عايش في بره؟

8. أيه الصراعات اللي كان بيعيشها في حياته؟

9. إزاي كانت نهايته؟ وأيه اللي حصل في مصر بعد وفاته؟

10. ليه ناس كتير شايفين إن عمر الشريف كان أكتر من مجرد ممثل؟

Discussion / Essay Prompts

1. هل ممكن فنان ينجح عالمياً من غير ما يغيّر هويته أو يفقد ارتباطه ببلده؟

2. في رأيك، الشهرة العالمية تستحق التضحية بالعلاقات الشخصية والحياة الخاصة؟ ناقش.

3. عمر الشريف كان "جسر بين حضارتين". هل شايف ده دور مهم للفن؟ ليه؟

صفية زغلول

Safiya Zaghloul played a powerful role in Egypt's struggle for independence. Known as "the Mother of the Egyptians," she earned deep respect for her leadership during a critical time in the nation's history. Her involvement in the 1919 revolution and her lifelong support for political and social progress made her a central figure in Egypt's national movement. She stood out as a strong voice for both freedom and women's participation in public life, leaving behind a legacy of courage, conviction, and commitment.

Pre-Reading Questions

1. أيه دور المرأه في الثورات والحركات الوطنية من وجهة نظرك؟

2. هل تعرف أسماء سيدات كان ليهم تأثير في تاريخ مصر؟ إحكي عن واحدة منهم.

3. هل شايف إن المرأة ممكن تكون قائدة سياسية بنفس كفاءة الراجل؟ ليه أو ليه لأ؟

Vocabulary

Read the definitions below. Each one matches a bold word or phrase in the text. Try to guess the terms first, then find them in context as you read. Answers are at the back of the book.

1. إن الست يكون ليها حرية وفرص متساوية في المجتمع

2. اسم بيت صفية وسعد زغلول، وكان مركز للنشاط السياسي

3. الكفاح علشان استقلال البلد وحرية الشعب

4. المشاركة في السياسة، أو الشغل، أو الحياة الاجتماعية

5. تسانده وتتكلم باسمه وتطلب حقوقه

6. تعاون بين اتنين أو أكتر في الكفاح السياسي أو الوطني

7. في قلب الحدث، مش واقف ورا أو متفرّج

8. كانت نموذج حقيقي وقدوة للناس

9. لقب لستّ الناس بتحبها وتحترمها علشان دورها الوطني

10. ناس من عائلات غنية وعندهم مكانة اجتماعية عالية

صفية زغلول: أم المصريين وقلب الثورة

لما نتكلم عن النضال الوطني في مصر، لازم نذكر صفية زغلول. مش بس علشان كانت مرات زعيم كبير، لكن علشان هي كمان كانت زعيمة، وصوت قوي للحرية والاستقلال. اتسمّت "أم المصريين"، والاسم ده ما كانش مجاملة، لكن تعبير عن حب واحترام شعب كامل ليها.

النشأة والتعليم

اتولدت صفية زغلول سنة ١٨٧٦، وكانت بنت مصطفى فهمي باشا، اللي كان وقتها رئيس وزراء مصر. يعني كانت من طبقة راقية، واتعلمت كويس في مدارس أجنبية، واتربّت على النظام والتقاليد الأرستقراطية.

رغم كده، ما كانتش شخصية متدلّعة أو بعيدة عن الواقع. بالعكس، كانت مثقفة، وبتحب تقرا، وعندها شخصية قوية. في سنة ١٨٩٦، اتجوزت سعد زغلول، اللي كان وقتها شاب طموح في بداية حياته السياسية.

شراكة نضالية مش بس زوجية

علاقة صفية بسعد ما كانتش مجرد جواز تقليدي. دول كانوا شركا حقيقيين في الفكر والنضال. كانت دايماً بتشارك في الحوارات السياسية اللي بتحصل في بيتهم، واللي كان دايماً مفتوح للمثقفين والسياسيين.

لما سعد بدأ يقود حركة وطنية ضد الاحتلال البريطاني، صفية ما كانتش في الخلفية... كانت في الصفوف الأمامية.

ثورة ١٩١٩ ودور صفية

لما الإنجليز نفوا سعد زغلول لمالطا في مارس ١٩١٩، مصر كلها انتفضت. الناس خرجت في مظاهرات، والستات لأول مرة نزلوا الشارع بأعداد كبيرة يهتفوا ضد

الاحتلال.

وكانت صفية زغلول في قلب المشهد. كانت بتنظم المظاهرات، وبتستقبل السيدات في بيت الأمة، وبتدعم الحركة بكل قوة. وجودها شجّع ستات كتير إنهم يشاركوا، وكان صوتها مسموع ومحترم.

البيت اللي كانت عايشة فيه بقى اسمه "بيت الأمة"، لأنه كان مركز للنشاط الوطني. وهناك كانت بتقابل الناس، وتخطط، وتكتب خطابات، وتتابع كل التفاصيل بنفسها.

أم المصريين

بعد ما الشعب شاف موقفها وشجاعتها، بدأوا ينادوها بـ"أم المصريين". اللقب ده ما جاش من فراغ. كانت بتتكلم باسم الشعب، وبتدافع عن قضيته، وبتضحي براحتها وخصوصيتها عشان الاستقلال.

فضلت صفية في دورها ده حتى بعد رجوع سعد من المنفى، وبعد ما بقى رئيس وزرا. وبعد وفاته سنة ١٩٢٧، ما انسحبتش من الساحة، لكن فضلت ناشطة وبتدافع عن مبادئه.

دورها في تمكين المرأة

صفية زغلول ما كانتش بس بتدافع عن حرية الوطن، لكن كمان عن دور الستات في المجتمع. كانت مؤمنة إن المرأة لازم يكون ليها صوت ودور في بناء البلد.

وجودها في السياسة شجّع ستات كتير يدخلوا المجال العام، سواء في السياسة أو التعليم أو العمل الاجتماعي. وكانت رمز للمرأة القوية اللي بتقدر تكون مثقفة، وطنية، وشجاعة في نفس الوقت.

السنين الأخيرة والميراث

في آخر سنين حياتها، عاشت صفية زغلول حياة هادية، لكن فضلت تتابع السياسة، وتستقبل زوّار في بيت الأمة. اتوفّت سنة ١٩٤٦، لكن ذكراها لسه عايشة.

صفية زغلول كانت نموذج نادر لست قوية، مثقفة، وطنية، ومحترمة من الكل. سابت بصمتها في التاريخ، وضربت مثل حيّ لكل الأجيال عن معنى المشاركة، والانتماء، والشجاعة.

Comprehension Questions

١. مين كانت صفية زغلول؟ وليه سموها "أم المصريين"؟

٢. كان أيه أصلها العائلي؟ واتعلمت فين؟

٣. إزاي كانت شراكتها مع سعد زغلول مش بس زوجية؟

٤. أيه دورها في ثورة ١٩١٩؟

٥. ليه الناس كانوا بيجتمعوا في "بيت الأمة"؟

٦. بعد وفاة سعد، صفية عملت أيه؟

٧. إزاي شجعت الستات على المشاركة في السياسة والمجتمع؟

٨. أيه الأفكار اللي كانت مؤمنة بيها عن دور المرأة؟

٩. اتكلم عن السنين الأخيرة من حياتها

١٠. ليه الناس لسه بتفتكرها لحد النهاردة؟

Discussion / Essay Prompts

١. في رأيك، أيه الصعوبات اللي بتواجه الستات اللي بيشاركوا في السياسة؟

٢. هل شايف إن تاريخ مصر أنصف الستات اللي لعبوا دور مهم؟ ناقش.

٣. أيه اللي ممكن نتعلمه من شخصية صفية زغلول النهارده؟

طه حسين

Taha Hussein is remembered not only as a writer but as a powerful voice for education, reason, and social progress. Despite losing his sight at a young age, he became a leading thinker in the Arab world and a symbol of determination and intellectual freedom. Through his work in literature and education, he challenged traditions and called for a more open and informed society. His life stands as a reminder that knowledge and critical thinking can break down barriers and change lives.

Pre-Reading Questions

1. في رأيك، هل التعليم ممكن يغيّر مصير شخص؟ عندك أمثلة من حياتك أو من ناس تعرفهم؟

2. أيه التحديات اللي ممكن تواجه الناس ذوي الإعاقة في المجتمع؟ إزاي ممكن نساعدهم يتغلبوا عليها؟

3. يعني أيه "حرية الفكر" بالنسبالك؟ وهل مهم يكون فيه نقاش واختلاف في الآراء في الجامعة أو في الإعلام؟

Vocabulary

Read the definitions below. Each one matches a bold word or phrase in the text. Try to guess the terms first, then find them in context as you read. Answers are at the back of the book.

١. إن الشخص ما يقدرش يشوف، سواء من ولادته أو بعدين

٢. إن الشخص يحس إنه جزء من المجتمع أو المكان اللي هو فيه

٣. إن الشخص يقدر يفكر ويعبّر عن رأيه من غير خوف أو ضغط

٤. استخدام التفكير والمنطق بدل العاطفة أو التقليد الأعمى

٥. تعبير مجازي، يعني إن الكلام أو الفكر ممكن يكون له تأثير قوي جداً على الناس والمجتمع

٦. حاجة قديمة ومش بتتغيّر بسهولة، عكس الحديث أو المتطور

٧. خطة هدفها نشر الوعي والثقافة والفكر الحر

٨. رفض آراء أو أفكار الآخرين لمجرد الاختلاف معاهم

٩. طريقة تعليم بتعتمد على الحفظ من غير فهم أو نقاش

١٠. يعمل تطوير في المناهج أو طريقة التدريس أو فرص التعليم

طه حسين: قُدرة العقل أقوى من البصر

لو فيه حد يستحق لقب "عميد الأدب العربي"، فهو طه حسين. مش بس لأنه كتب كتب مهمة، لكن لأنه كان صاحب مشروع تنويري كبير، هدفه ينهض بالمجتمع من خلال التعليم والثقافة. وهو كمان كان مثال حيّ على إن الإعاقة مش نهاية، لكن بداية لحكاية عظيمة.

الطفولة وفقدان البصر

اتولد طه حسين سنة ١٨٨٩ في قرية صغيرة اسمها عزبة الكيلو، في محافظة المنيا، في صعيد مصر. لما كان عنده حوالي ٣ سنين، أصيب بالرمد، وعشان مكنش فيه علاج كويس وقتها، فقد بصره تماماً. ورغم كده، ما استسلمش، وكان دايماً فضولي وذكي، بيحب يسمع ويحفظ كل حاجة.

أبوه كان موظف بسيط، وكان عنده ١٣ أخ وأخت. ورغم إن الظروف ما كانتش سهلة، دخل طه حسين الكُتّاب وحفظ القرآن كامل وهو طفل صغير. حفظه للقرآن ساعده جداً في تقوية لغته وحفظه، وده ظهر في أسلوبه بعدين.

من الأزهر لفرنسا

بعد ما خلص الكُتّاب، راح طه حسين القاهرة ودخل الأزهر، وبدأ يدرس الفقه، والنحو، والحديث. بس بعد فترة، بدأ يحس إن التعليم هناك تقليدي ومش بيشجّع على التفكير الحر. ولما افتتحوا جامعة القاهرة (وقتها كانت اسمها الجامعة الأهلية) سنة ١٩٠٨، انضم ليها، وكان من أوائل الطلبة فيها.

في الجامعة، اتعرّف على أساتذة مصريين وأجانب، وبدأ يوسّع تفكيره، ويتعمق في الأدب والتاريخ والفلسفة. وكتب رسالة الدكتوراه بتاعته عن "أبو العلاء المعري"، وقال فيها رأيه بصراحة، وده خلى ناس كتير تهاجمه، لكن هو ما خافش، واتمسّك بحقه في حرية الفكر.

في سنة ١٩١٤، راح فرنسا عشان يكمّل دراسته، وهناك قابل "سوزان" اللي بقت مراته بعد كده، وكانت هي اللي ساعدته يندمج في الحياة هناك، وكانت بتقرا له الكتب، وتترجم له. درس في جامعة السوربون، وخد دكتوراه تانية في الأدب.

التعليم والتغيير

لما رجع مصر، اشتغل أستاذ في جامعة القاهرة، وبعد كده بقى عميد كلية الآداب، وبعدين وزير للمعارف (اللي هي دلوقتي وزارة التعليم). في الفترة دي، حاول يغيّر شكل التعليم في مصر.

قال إن "التعليم زي الميّه والهوا"، حق لكل مواطن"، وكان مؤمن إن مصر مش هتتقدم إلا لما كل الناس تتعلم، سواء غني أو فقير، راجل أو ست.

طه حسين شجّع على تعليم البنات، وعلى تدريس الأدب والفكر النقدي، مش بس الحفظ والتلقين. وكان بيحاول دايماً يخلّي الجامعة مكان حر للبحث والنقاش، مش مجرد شهادة.

كتبه وأفكاره

كتب طه حسين كتب كتير، من أشهرها:

○ الأيام: وده سيرة ذاتية عن طفولته وحياته
○ في الشعر الجاهلي: وده كتاب عمل ضجة كبيرة، لأنه ناقش أصل الشعر العربي بطريقة جديدة
○ مستقبل الثقافة في مصر: وده كتاب عن علاقة التعليم بالنهضة
○ حديث الأربعاء: مقالات في الأدب والنقد

كانت أفكاره دايماً بتدور حوالين العقلانية، الحرية، وحق الإنسان في السؤال والتفكير. وكان مؤمن إن الأدب مش بس كلام جميل، لكنه وسيلة لفهم النفس والمجتمع.

التحديات والهجوم

بسبب أفكاره الجريئة، اتعرض طه حسين لهجوم كبير من ناس كتير، سواء من رجال دين أو سياسيين أو حتى أدباء. بعض الناس شتموه، وبعضهم حاولوا يمنعوا كتبه.

لكنّه كان ثابت على مبادئه، ودايماً بيرد بالحجة والمنطق. ما كانش بيحب الصدام، لكنه كمان ما كانش بيقبل السكوت على الجهل أو التعصّب.

رغم كل الهجوم، أصبح طه حسين واحد من أهم المفكرين اللي غيّروا طريقة الناس في التفكير.

نهايته وميراثه

فضل طه حسين يكتب لحد آخر عمره، رغم كِبر السن وتعب الجسد. مات سنة ١٩٧٣، بس لحد النهاردة، اسمه لسه بينور أي نقاش عن التعليم، الثقافة، أو الحرية.

هو ما كانش بس كاتب أو وزير، هو كان حلم ماشي على الأرض، حلم إن كل طفل في قرية صغيرة يقدر يوصل للجامعة، حتى لو ما بيشوفش.

طه حسين هو دليل حي إن العقل أقوى من أي إعاقة، وإن الكلمة ممكن تغيّر مجتمع كامل.

Comprehension Questions

١. طه حسين اتولد فين؟ وأيه اللي حصل له وهو صغير؟

٢. إزاي فقد البصر أثّر على طريقة تفكيره وتعلمه؟

٣. ليه ما كانش مرتاح في الأزهر؟ وراح فين بعد كده؟

٤. أيه الموضوع اللي كتب عنه رسالته في الدكتوراه؟ وأيه اللي حصل بسببها؟

٥. مين سوزان؟ وإزاي ساعدته في فرنسا؟

٦. لما رجع مصر، اشتغل فين؟ وأيه المناصب اللي وصل لها؟

٧. أيه رأيه في التعليم؟ وإزاي حاول يطوّره؟

٨. اذكر كتابين من كتبه، وقول باختصار هما عن أيه.

٩. ليه ناس كتير كانوا بيهاجموه؟ وإزاي كان بيرد عليهم؟

١٠. في رأيك، أيه اللي خلى طه حسين يفضل مؤثر لحد النهاردة؟

Discussion / Essay Prompts

١. أيه رأيك في جملة "التعليم زي الميّة والهوا"، حق لكل مواطن؟ هل ده متطبّق فعلاً في مصر؟

٢. لو كنت مسؤول عن تطوير التعليم في بلدك، هتبدأ منين؟

٣. هل شايف إن فيه كتاب أو مفكرين النهاردة بيكملوا طريق طه حسين؟ ليه أو ليه لأ؟

عمر خيـرت

Omar Khairat has shaped a musical style that speaks without words and reaches straight to the heart. Blending classical training with Egyptian soul, he created a sound that feels both personal and universal. His melodies have become part of daily life for many Egyptians, marking quiet moments and major memories alike. As a composer and performer, Khairat continues to inspire new generations and hold a special place in the cultural life of the Arab world.

Pre-Reading Questions

1. هل بتحب تسمع موسيقى من غير غنا؟ أيه اللي ممكن يخلي الموسيقى "تتكلم"؟

2. في رأيك، أيه دور الموسيقى في التعبير عن الهوية الثقافية؟

3. هل حضرت حفلة موسيقية كلاسيكية أو حفلة لعمر خيرت قبل كده؟ شارك تجربتك.

Vocabulary

Read the definitions below. Each one matches a bold word or phrase in the text. Try to guess the terms first, then find them in context as you read. Answers are at the back of the book.

١. إحساس أو مزاج عام بيخلقه الفنان من خلال فنه

٢. الحاجات اللي بتميز الشخصية والثقافة المصرية

٣. ترتيب الآلات والأنغام في أغنية أو مقطوعة موسيقية

٤. حاجة نادرة ومميزة وصعب تتكرر بنفس الشكل

٥. حفلة أو مكان مليان ناس ومفيش مكان فاضي

٦. شخص أو فكرة بتشجّع وتحمّس الناس على الإبداع

٧. مشاعر وأحاسيس عميقة جوا الإنسان

٨. موسيقى بتتعرض في الخلفية في الأفلام أو المسلسلات علشان توضح المشاعر

٩. نوع موسيقى عربي قديم بيعتمد على الإحساس والكلام العميق

١٠. وجود دائم ومؤثر في الساحة الفنية أو في قلوب الناس

عُمر خيــرت: أنغــام بتحكي من غير كلام

أول ما تسمع لحن من ألحانه، تحس إنك دخلت عالم مختلف. عمر خيرت قدر يخلق لنفسه أسلوب موسيقي مميز، بيجمع بين الإحساس الراقي والهوية المصرية. من غير ما يغني، بيعرف يوصّل مشاعر وحكايات، ويلمس وجدان الناس بنغمة بسيطة أو لحن معبّر. موسيقاه بقت جزء من ذوق المصريين، وحاضرة في لحظات كتير من حياتهم.

البدايات: بيت كله موسيقى

اتولد عمر خيرت سنة ١٩٤٨، في بيت فني في حي السيدة زينب في القاهرة. كان جده، محمود خيرت، موسيقي ومؤلف معروف، وأخوه كمان كان عازف بيانو.

من صغره كان فيه موسيقى حواليه، فكان طبيعي إنه يتجه للمجال ده. بدأ يتعلم بيانو وهو طفل، وبعد كده درس في معهد الكونسرفتوار في القاهرة، وركّز على الموسيقى الكلاسيكية الغربية.

بس رغم دراسته الكلاسيكية، كان دايماً عنده شغف إنه يدمج الإحساس المصري في اللي بيعزفه.

من فرقة إلى نجم

في شبابه، كان عضو في فرقة موسيقية اسمها "Les Petits Chats"، ودي كانت من أشهر الفرق الغربية في مصر في الستينات. التجربة دي عرّفته على جمهور مختلف، وخلّته أقرب للناس.

بعد كده، بدأ يتّجه للموسيقى التصويرية، وابتدى يألف لمسرحيات وأفلام. ودي كانت بداية مرحلة جديدة في حياته، خلت اسمه يبقى مرتبط بمشاعر المصريين.

موسيقاه: قصة من غير كلمات

اللي يميّز عمر خيرت إن موسيقاه بتقول كلام من غير ما تتكلم. بتسمع ألحانه وتحس بحزن، فرح، حنين، أو حتى توتر. بيعرف يستخدم الآلات علشان يرسم حالة كاملة.

في أعماله، تلاقي تأثيرات من موسيقى الجاز، والموسيقى الكلاسيكية، والطرب الشرقي الأصيل. بيخلط كل ده في أسلوبه الخاص، اللي مفيش زيه.

كتير من الناس ما بيحبوش يسمعوا موسيقى من غير غنا، لكن لما يسمعوا عمر خيرت، بيحسوا إنهم فهموا القصة من غير ولا كلمة.

أعمال مشهورة خَلّت اسمه أيقونة

من أشهر أعماله:

- موسيقى "ضمير أبلة حكمت"
- موسيقى "وجه القمر"
- موسيقى "الخواجة عبد القادر"
- موسيقى فيلم "البحث عن سيد مرزوق"
- موسيقى "اللقاء الثاني"
- توزيع موسيقي جديد لأغاني أم كلثوم وعبد الحليم حافظ

أعماله ما بتتنسيش، وكل حفلة ليه بتبقى كاملة العدد. ناس من كل الأعمار بيجوا يسمعوه، وكتير منهم بيبقوا حافظين الألحان زي الأغاني بالظبط.

حفلاته: تجربة ما تتكررش

حفلات عمر خيرت مش بس موسيقى، دي تجربة كاملة. المسرح بيبقى منور، الجمهور ساكت وهو بيسمع، وكل نغمة بتلمس حاجة جوا الناس.

كتير من الناس بيقولوا إنهم راحوا حفلة ليه وخرجوا وهمّ متأثّرين جداً، كأنهم عاشوا فيلم أو حلم. وده بيوضح قد أيه فنه بيأثر في وجدان الناس.

التأثير والتعليم

عمر خيرت مش بس فنان بيقدّم أعمال، لكنه كمان مصدر إلهام لموسيقيين شباب. كتير من اللي بيدرسوا موسيقى في مصر والعالم العربي بياخدوه قدوة.

كمان ساهم في رفع قيمة الموسيقى اللي بدون غنا في العالم العربي، وخلّى ناس كتير تحب تسمعها لأول مرة في حياتهم.

حضور مستمر في قلوب الناس

رغم مرور السنين، لسه عمر خيرت محافظ على مكانته. كل حفلة ليه بتبقى ترند، وكل مشروع جديد بيثير الحماس.

الناس بتحبه مش بس علشان فنه، لكن كمان علشان تواضعه، احترامه للجمهور، واستمراره في العطاء من غير توقف.

Comprehension Questions

1. أيه اللي بيميز موسيقى عمر خيرت عن باقي المؤلفين الموسيقيين؟

2. اتولد فين؟ وأيه اللي خلّاه يحب الموسيقى من صغره؟

3. ازاي كانت بدايته الفنية؟ وأيه الفرقة اللي انضم ليها؟

4. ليه موسيقاه بتوصل للناس من غير كلمات؟

5. أيه أنواع الموسيقى اللي بيخلطها عمر خيرت في أعماله؟

6. اذكر ٣ من أشهر أعماله الموسيقية.

7. أيه اللي بيخلي حفلاته مميزة؟

8. إزاي أثّر عمر خيرت في الشباب اللي بيدرسوا موسيقى؟

9. ليه ناس كتير بيعتبروه رمز فني مش مجرد مؤلف موسيقي؟

10. إزاي حافظ على نجاحه وشعبيته على مر السنين؟

Discussion / Essay Prompts

1. تفتكر إن الموسيقى من غير غنا ليها تأثير أقوى من الأغاني؟ ناقش بمثال.

2. في رأيك، إزاي ممكن نستخدم الموسيقى علشان نحافظ على هويتنا الثقافية؟

3. ناقش تأثير عمر خيرت على المشهد الموسيقي في مصر والعالم العربي.

Vocabulary Answer Key

Naguib Mahfouz

6. صارم	1. يتصادر
7. سهل ممتنع	2. الطبقة المتوسطة
8. جُواه حب حقيقي	3. القهاوي
9. وعيه	4. ميراث ضخم
10. صدام	5. مؤرخ اجتماعي

Yousra

6. تمسّ الناس	1. جيل ورا جيل
7. تحقّق نفسها	2. محافظة على صورتها
8. جزء من الذاكرة الفنية	3. ثُنائي
9. سفيرة نوايا حسنة	4. توصل مشاعر
10. أيقونة في الفن	5. كيميا حقيقية

Rifa'a al-Tahtawi

6. صدمة حضارية	1. مبادئ
7. نقطة تحوّل	2. تقليد أعمى
8. بعثة تعليمية	3. الأصالة والتجديد
9. مدرسة الألسن	4. نهضة
10. يبسّط المفاهيم	5. قدوة ومُلهِم

Gamal Abdel Nasser

٦. حرب الاستنزاف	١. كرامة وطنية
٧. القومية العربية	٢. التأميم
٨. خطاب تاريخي	٣. صمد
٩. الظباط الأحرار	٤. النكسة
١٠. يتنحى	٥. العدوان الثلاثي

Rania Al-Mashat

٦. صندوق النقد الدولي	١. الشفافية
٧. التنمية المستدامة	٢. برامج إصلاح اقتصادي
٨. التفاوض	٣. حضور
٩. مؤسسات دولية	٤. صورة عصرية
١٠. منصة التعاون التنسيقي	٥. السياسات النقدية

Mohamed Salah

٦. رمز للأمل	١. لمع نجمه
٧. قدوة	٢. شغله على نفسه
٨. لسه المشوار مكمل	٣. الطريق ما كانش سهل
٩. تحدي كبير	٤. النجاح مش صدفة
١٠. يثبت نفسه	٥. النقلة الكبيرة

Umm Kulthum

6. وطنية	1. راقية
7. تفاعل الجمهور	2. شاعرية
8. فراق	3. النكسة
9. جنازة	4. الكرامة
10. سمّيعة	5. الكوبليه

Magdi Yacoub

6. تخصص	1. عمته
7. قدوة	2. واجب مش فضل
8. تقنيات حديثة	3. تواضع
9. علاج مجاني	4. الغُربة
10. أجرى عمليات	5. بيسيب بصمة

Omar Sharif

6. ساب وراه تاريخ طويل	1. جسر بين الشرق والغرب
7. قصة حب كانت حديث الناس	2. اتغيّرت حياته تماماً
8. صراعات داخلية	3. رحلته كانت مليانة تحديات
9. شهرة ضخمة	4. فتح له أبوابه
10. يقلّل من التمثيل	5. رمز لجيل كامل

Safiya Zaghloul

6. شراكة نضالية		1. تمكين المرأة	
7. الصفوف الأمامية		2. بيت الأمة	
8. ضربت مثل حيّ		3. النضال الوطني	
9. أم المصريين		4. المجال العام	
10. طبقة راقية		5. تدافع عن قضيته	

Taha Hussein

6. التقليدي		1. فقدان البصر	
7. مشروع تنويري		2. يندمج	
8. التعصّب		3. حرية الفكر	
9. التلقين		4. العقلانية	
10. يغيّر شكل التعليم		5. كلمة تغيّر مجتمع	

Omar Khairat

6. مصدر إلهام		1. حالة كاملة	
7. وجدان الناس		2. الهوية المصرية	
8. موسيقى تصويرية		3. توزيع موسيقي	
9. الطرب الشرقي الأصيل		4. تجربة ما تتكررش	
10. حضور مستمر		5. كاملة العدد	

Translations

Naguib Mahfouz

Naguib Mahfouz: The Storyteller of Egypt

Naguib Mahfouz is one of the most famous writers Egypt has ever produced in the 20th century. Many people say he's not just a writer; he's a social and cultural historian of Egypt. He wrote about the people, the streets, the alleyways, the coffee houses, the dreams and the hardships. Anyone who reads his work feels like they're walking through the old streets of Cairo themselves.

Childhood and Beginnings

Naguib Mahfouz was born in the neighborhood of Al-Gamaleya, in the heart of Cairo, in 1911. That neighborhood was full of life: the voices of street vendors, the smell of food from the houses, the sound of the call to prayer, and kids playing in the alleyways. This life entered his heart early on and stayed with him his whole life, and you can clearly see it in his writing.

He was the youngest of his siblings, and that meant he spent a lot of his childhood alone at home. So, he found himself spending long hours reading. He loved to read everything: stories, religious books, history, and also European literature. That's how his identity as a writer began to take shape.

After finishing school, he enrolled in the Faculty of Arts at Cairo University, majoring in Philosophy. That was not a typical choice at the time, but Naguib had a genuine love for thought and reflection.

From Philosophy to Literature

After graduating, he worked as a government employee and moved between ministries. Even though the job took up a lot of his time, he always managed to make time to write. At first, he wrote short stories, then moved on to full-length novels.

In the beginning, he was influenced by ancient Egyptian history, and wrote novels like The Struggle of Thebes and Fate's Mockery. But later on, he shifted from history to reality—to the people around him, the middle and lower classes, and a Cairo that was changing day by day.

The Trilogy and a Turning Point

His most famous work is The Cairo Trilogy: Palace Walk, Palace of Desire, and Sugar Street. These novels tell the story of an ordinary Egyptian family, from the time of British occupation up to after the 1952 revolution. The characters are incredibly realistic: the strict father, the kind mother, and the children, each following a different path in life.

This trilogy isn't just about one family; it's a mirror of all of Egypt during that time. That's why many people consider it one of the greatest literary works in the Arab world.

His Writing Style

Naguib Mahfouz's style is deceptively simple. His sentences are straightforward, but full of depth. His characters talk like everyday people, but their ideas carry philosophy and deep questions about life, death, freedom, religion, and love.

He also had a rare gift for describing places. When you read his work, you can smell the street, hear the cars, and see the colors of the buildings. He didn't just write stories; he made the reader live them.

Politics and Censorship

Even though Mahfouz wasn't a political activist, he wrote about important political and social issues. In his novels, you'll find criticism of corruption, dictatorship, and extremism. That's why some of his works were banned or censored at times.

His novel Children of the Alley (Awlād Ḥāritnā), for example, faced huge backlash. He was accused of insulting religion, even though he repeatedly stated that wasn't his intention. The controversy reached a point where someone tried to assassinate him in the 1990s and stabbed him in the neck.

Still, Mahfouz wasn't confrontational. He remained calm, believed in freedom of thought, but didn't like provocation.

Nobel Prize and Global Recognition

In 1988, Naguib Mahfouz won the Nobel Prize in Literature. That was a historic event; he was the first Arab writer to receive that honor. Suddenly, the whole world started talking about him, and his works were translated into many languages.

But Naguib remained humble and simple. He didn't seek fame. He stayed in the same apartment, went to the same coffe house, and talked to the same friends.

A Quiet Ending and a Lasting Legacy

In his final years, his health began to decline, especially after the assassination attempt. It became difficult for him to write by hand, so he started dictating stories to a close friend. And he kept writing until the very end.

Naguib Mahfouz died in 2006, at the age of 94. But he's still alive in people's hearts and in the pages of his books, which are still being read and studied today.

He wasn't just a writer; he was a living archive of Egypt in the 20th century. That's why anyone who wants to understand Egypt must read Naguib Mahfouz.

Yousra

Yousra: Many Faces... But One Heart

Yousra holds a special place in the hearts of Egyptians and Arabs. Her talent, charisma, and elegance have made her one of the most important stars in the Arab arts scene for over forty years. She has balanced a wide range of roles with a steady career, consistently offering performances that resonate with people and reflect their lives with honesty.

Early Beginnings

Her real name is Civene Hafez Nassim, and she was born in 1955. She began her acting career in the late 1970s, starting out in small film roles. But she quickly drew attention thanks to her unique screen presence.

Although she was very beautiful, she didn't rely on looks alone. She worked hard on her craft, improved her skills, and chose roles that showcased her real talent.

Her Big Break

In the 1980s, Yousra began working with the legendary director Youssef Chahine, which marked a turning point in her career. She acted in films like Egyptian Story and Alexandria Again and Forever, which introduced a new side of her to the audience: intellectual, thoughtful, and different.

She also formed a long and beloved partnership with actor Adel Imam. Together they starred in many successful films, such as The Human and the Jinn, Karakoon in the Street, and Terrorism and Kebab. Audiences loved seeing them together. They had real chemistry on screen.

Television and Popularity at Home

Yousra didn't stop at cinema. She also achieved great success in television. Her TV series have always touched people emotionally and entered their homes with ease.

Some of her most well-known series include:

- Where Is My Heart?
- A Matter of Public Opinion
- Critical Moments
- Betrayal of a Promise
- Civil War

Her roles were always diverse: a mother, a wife, a judge, a doctor, or a woman facing life's challenges. She consistently conveyed emotion in a way that was simple and heartfelt.

Yousra the Person

Away from acting, Yousra is known for her kindness and humility. She takes part in many charity initiatives and supports causes like women's rights, cancer awareness, and education.

She's also a UN Goodwill Ambassador, and participates in cultural and humanitarian events in Egypt and across the Arab world. She uses her fame to help others, not to show off.

A Modern Female Role Model

To many, Yousra isn't just an actress. She's a role model for strong, successful women who've earned public respect. She's never been caught in scandal, always maintains her image, and speaks with wisdom and calm.

Her clothing, her words, and her choices reflect refined taste and awareness. Because of this, she has become an icon in art, fashion, and public life.

Yousra and the Younger Generation

Despite her long time in the spotlight, Yousra still has a huge following among young people. She knows how to reinvent herself, work with new directors and actors, and reach different generations.

Her TV appearances during Ramadan are something people look forward to every year. She always has something new to offer, whether in her acting or public positions.

Her Legacy and Influence

Throughout her career, Yousra has maintained her unique presence and become part of the cultural memory of Egypt and the Arab world. Generation after generation continues to love and follow her, because she knows how to connect with people simply and remain close to their hearts.

Rifa'a al-Tahtawi

Rifa'a al-Tahtawi: The Beginning of Modern Egypt

Rifa'a al-Tahtawi played a major role in shaping modern Egypt during the 19th century. He was a scholar, translator, educator, and reformer whose work opened the door to a new way of thinking. Through his efforts to introduce modern sciences, develop education, and promote cultural exchange, he helped build a foundation for progress that blended tradition with renewal.

From Upper Egypt to Al-Azhar

Rifa'a was born in 1801 in the city of Tahta in Upper Egypt. From a young age, he loved reading and learning, and his family encouraged him to attend Al-Azhar in Cairo. There, he studied Islamic law, language, and interpretation, and he was one of the top students.

At Al-Azhar, he was influenced by several open-minded teachers, and he had a slightly different way of thinking than most students. He wasn't satisfied with memorizing. He always asked questions and tried to understand the deeper meaning behind things.

His Journey to France: A Cultural Shock

In 1826, while still a young man, he was chosen to travel to France with the first Egyptian educational mission sent by Mohamed Ali Pasha. At first, he went as the mission's religious leader, but over time, he started learning French and immersing himself in European culture.

He spent about five years there, studying philosophy, politics, engineering, and modern sciences. Everything he saw was new to him—how schools worked, the importance of laws, the role of women, and how much people valued knowledge.

That trip became a turning point in his life, and he returned to Egypt with a completely different view of the world.

Translating Ideas, Not Just Words

When he came back to Egypt, he began working in translation. But he wasn't just converting words from one language to another; he was transferring ideas, principles, and a new way of seeing the world.

He worked at the School of Medicine and later at The School of Languages (Madrasat al-Alsun), helping translate books in a wide range of fields: history, geography, science, and politics. He always tried to make complex ideas easier to understand and chose his Arabic terms carefully to suit the Egyptian reader.

Education at the Heart of His Mission

Rifa'a believed that Egypt couldn't rise without education. That's why he dedicated himself to developing curricula and helping create new schools, not only for boys but also for girls. He saw women's education not as a threat but as a foundation for building a stronger society.

He also focused on training teachers, organizing schools, and writing educational books in Arabic that were completely new to Egyptians at the time.

A Cultural Project, Not Just Academic Work

Beyond education, Rifa'a had a much broader cultural vision. He wanted to build a balance: to benefit from Western civilization without blindly copying it, and at the same time, to preserve Islamic and Arab identity.

He didn't see any contradiction between religion and science or between tradition and progress. He always worked to open doors for dialogue and to persuade people to evolve through understanding, not confrontation.

Challenges and Political Setbacks

Even though his work was focused on culture and education, he couldn't avoid politics. He held several official positions and was close to decision-makers. But at times, his ideas weren't welcomed by everyone in power. As a result, he was removed or sidelined from his roles more than once.

Still, even during difficult periods, he held on to his principles and kept working—in education, translation, and writing.

A Legacy That Lives On

Rifa'a al-Tahtawi passed away in 1873, but his impact continues to this day. Many schools founded after him followed the model he helped shape. Generations of intellectuals have seen him as a role model and source of inspiration, both in the 19th century and beyond.

His ideas about education, women's rights, the relationship between religion and science, and the importance of translation have become part of cultural discussions across Egypt and the Arab world.

The First Step in a Long Journey

What Rifa'a did wasn't a full revolution, but it was the first step on the path to change. He opened new doors and got people thinking in a different way.

He spent his life believing that knowledge and moral upbringing were the foundation of progress, and that the Egyptian people deserved an education that would help them rise and stand confidently among the nations of the world.

Gamal Abdel Nasser

Gamal Abdel Nasser: Leader of the Revolution and Voice of Dignity

Gamal Abdel Nasser was one of the most influential figures in modern Egyptian history. He was born at a time when Egypt was still under British influence, and he grew up witnessing injustice, poverty, and inequality. All of these experiences were the beginning of a long journey of change and struggle for national dignity.

Early Life and Growing Awareness

Nasser was born in 1918 in the Bakos neighborhood of Alexandria, though his family originally came from Beni Suef Governorate. His father was a modest postal worker, and because of frequent transfers, Nasser spent his childhood in several different cities.

Even as a child, he was interested in politics. He joined protests against the occupation, and he read newspapers and books about independence and revolution. In 1937, he enrolled in the Military Academy, where he met other officers who shared his ideas. And together they began to dream of real change in the country.

The July 23, 1952 Revolution

After years of corruption, a growing gap between rich and poor, and continued British domination, Nasser and a group of fellow officers (who later became known as the Free Officers) planned a military coup. On the night of July 23, 1952, they took control of key locations in Cairo and forced King Farouk to abdicate.

At first, Mohamed Naguib served as the official leader of the Revolutionary Command Council. But after internal conflicts, Nasser became the real leader. In 1956, he was formally elected President of Egypt.

The Nationalization of the Suez Canal

One of the most defining moments in Nasser's career came on July 26, 1956, when he gave a historic speech announcing the nationalization of the Suez Canal. This decision came after the US and Britain refused to finance Egypt's Aswan High Dam project, so Nasser decided to use the canal's revenues to fund the project himself.

The reaction was swift and severe. Britain, France, and Israel launched a military attack on Egypt in October 1956, in what became known as the Tripartite Aggression. But the Egyptian people stood strong, and international support (especially from the United States and the Soviet Union) forced the invading forces to withdraw.

The nationalization was a huge blow to colonial powers and turned Nasser into a national hero, not just in Egypt but across the entire Arab world.

Arab Unity and the Nationalist Dream

Nasser dreamed of a united Arab world, a strong bloc of Arab nations working together. In 1958, Egypt and Syria formed a political union called the United Arab Republic, but it only lasted three years.

Even though the union failed, the idea of Arab nationalism stayed alive. Nasser saw the liberation of Palestine, the end of colonialism, and shared Arab economic development as essential goals the Arab world needed to pursue together.

His speeches were always powerful and inspiring. He spoke to people in simple language that touched their hearts; and that's what made millions love and follow him.

The Setback and Defiance

In June 1967, Egypt suffered a major setback when Israel launched a surprise attack on Egypt, Syria, and Jordan, occupying Sinai, the West Bank, and the Golan Heights. The defeat was a huge shock, and many blamed Nasser.

On June 9, Nasser gave a speech announcing his resignation. But the very next day, millions of Egyptians took to the streets chanting that he must stay. Moved by this overwhelming support, he decided to stay on.

Despite the defeat, Nasser began rebuilding the Egyptian army and launched the War of Attrition, preparing the country for a future battle to liberate Sinai.

Death and Legacy

On September 28, 1970, Gamal Abdel Nasser died suddenly of a heart attack. He was only 52 years old. His death shocked the entire Arab world, and millions attended his funeral in Cairo.

Though people have differing opinions about Nasser, no one can deny that he transformed Egypt. He made national dignity and social justice legitimate demands.

To this day, people still listen to his speeches, remember his positions, and talk about "the era of Abdel Nasser."

Rania Al-Mashat

Rania Al-Mashat: Economics, Diplomacy, and Empowerment

Rania Al-Mashat is one of the prominent faces in Egypt's recent political and economic life. She's known for her presence, confidence, and communication style that blends seriousness with diplomacy. She has reached high-level positions and become a role model for educated, ambitious Egyptian women who can represent their country on the world stage.

Early Life and Education

Rania was born in 1975 and grew up in a household that valued education. From a young age, she was drawn to numbers, analysis, and big questions about the economy and society. She studied economics at the American University in Cairo, where she was consistently one of the top students.

After graduation, she continued her studies in the United States, earning a master's and PhD in economics from the University of Maryland. Her academic focus was on macroeconomics, monetary policy, and global markets.

Central Bank of Egypt and the IMF

She returned to Egypt and worked at the Central Bank of Egypt in the monetary policy department. There, she helped develop new tools and contributed to modernizing the country's economic strategy.

Later, she joined the International Monetary Fund (IMF) in Washington, becoming one of the youngest Egyptians to reach the role of economic advisor. She took part in negotiations with various countries and traveled to many places to help design economic reform programs.

These years were critical in shaping her personality as an analyst and strengthening her experience in crisis management and government negotiations.

Minister of Tourism in a Challenging Time

In 2018, she was appointed as Minister of Tourism, a challenging period, as Egypt's tourism industry was still recovering from the aftermath of 2011.

Rania Al-Mashat took a fresh approach. She focused on modernizing Egypt's image and launched a campaign called "People to People" to show the world not just the monuments, but the beauty of Egyptian people. She also launched the "Experience Egypt" campaign, using social media in a smart and modern way to promote a positive image globally.

She invested in training tourism workers and improving service quality, helping tourism gradually recover.

Ministry of International Cooperation

In 2020, she became the Minister of International Cooperation, a role that requires a careful balance of diplomacy, economics, and negotiation. Her job involves managing Egypt's relationships with international institutions like the World Bank, the European Union, and development agencies.

Rania works to align financing with sustainable development, meaning that external funding isn't just about loans; it's used for projects that benefit people: schools, hospitals, renewable energy, and infrastructure.

She launched the "Joint Coordination Cooperation Platform" to streamline cooperation between the government and international partners. She always emphasizes transparency and communication, publishing public reports on all projects and figures.

Representing Egypt Internationally

Rania represents Egypt at major conferences around the world, from the United Nations to the World Economic Forum in Davos. She speaks fluent English and knows how to present Egypt's position in a clear and convincing way.

Many international media outlets have described her as a modern face of Egypt, seeing in her a model of a woman capable of handling complex issues with confidence and skill.

Her Style and Communication

People have noticed her distinctive style: elegant attire, clear language, and a well-organized way of speaking. She always relies on numbers, values transparency, and answers questions directly.

She's also active on social media, especially X (formerly known as Twitter), which she uses to share her work, highlight her ministry's achievements, and post photos from visits and meetings.

Her Legacy and Influence

Rania Al-Mashat is still in the prime of her career, but her impact is already clear. She has reshaped the image of women in ministerial roles and set an example of leadership grounded in knowledge and professionalism.

Many young women see her as a source of inspiration, and many believe that Egypt needs more leaders like her: organized, transparent, and focused on long-term results.

Mohamed Salah

Mohamed Salah: From the Village of Nagrig to Global Fame

Mohamed Salah is no longer just a soccer star; he has become a symbol of hope, ambition, and hard work that leads to success. Every child in Egypt now sees in him a real example that dreams can come true, no matter how humble the beginning.

Starting Out in Nagrig

Mohamed Salah was born in 1992 in a village called Nagrig, in Gharbia Governorate. A simple village, a modest home, and an ordinary family. From a young age, he was crazy about soccer. He played in the streets, at school, anywhere he could find space.

His family always supported him, but the road wasn't easy. To get to training at El Mokawloon (Arab Contractors) Club in Cairo, he had to wake up very early, take multiple buses, and come back exhausted at night, but he never complained.

Playing Professionally in Europe

After making a name for himself at El Mokawloon, he got an offer from the Swiss club Basel in 2012. Moving abroad was a huge challenge. He didn't know the language, the customs, or the atmosphere. But Salah had a remarkable determination, and he focused on one goal: to succeed.

From Basel, he transferred to Chelsea, but he didn't get much of a chance there. Many people thought he wouldn't make it, but he was determined to prove himself. He went on loan to Fiorentina, then to Roma, and that's where people really started to notice him.

In 2017 came the big leap when he joined Liverpool. From his very first season, he became the star of the team, broke records, and won many awards, including the Premier League Golden Boot.

His Work Ethic

What sets Mohamed Salah apart isn't just his talent; it's his constant effort. He's always keeping up his fitness, training more than expected, paying attention to his diet and sleep, and staying out of trouble in his personal life.

He's calm, humble, and always smiling. And that's made people love him not just in Egypt, but all over the world. His fans in England sing for him in the stadiums, and kids across the Arab world hang his photos on their walls.

Pride of Egypt and the Arabs

Mohamed Salah isn't just a soccer player; he's become a symbol of Egypt. When he plays for the national team, everyone watches. He played a huge role in helping Egypt qualify for the 2018 World Cup after a long absence. People were crying with joy. And Salah was at the heart of that moment.

He also constantly returns to his village, helps the people there, and donates to hospitals, schools, and mosques. He hasn't forgotten where he came from, and that's made people respect him even more.

Success Is No Accident

Mohamed Salah's story teaches us that success doesn't come by chance. He worked hard, was patient, stumbled and got back up, and kept chasing his dream. He always says that failure isn't the end, and that every day is a new opportunity.

Young people in Egypt and the Arab world now see him as a role model, not just in soccer, but in character, ambition, and determination.

The Journey Isn't Over

Salah is still young, with many years ahead of him on the field. But even if he were to retire tomorrow, his impact would remain. He showed an entire generation that a boy from a small village can shine in the biggest stadiums.

He's not just the pride of Egypt; he's the pride of the Arab world, and of anyone who believes that dreams can come true if you back them up with real effort.

Umm Kulthum

Umm Kulthum: The Voice of Egypt and the Arab World

If there's one voice we can truly call "the voice of Egypt," it would be, without question, Umm Kulthum. The woman who grew up in a small village and later became an icon of Arab art, not just in Egypt, but across every Arabic-speaking country. Her voice carried strength and emotion, and the lyrics of her songs were full of poetry, patriotism, and love.

Childhood and Early Beginnings

Umm Kulthum was born around 1904 in a small village called Tammay al-Zahayra in the Dakahlia governorate. Her father was a religious teacher who taught children the Qur'an, and she also began memorizing the Qur'an at a young age. Her voice was strong and clear, and eventually her father began taking her with him to perform religious songs and simple celebrations.

At first, people didn't know she was a girl, because she wore boys' clothes when singing; at the time, society didn't accept the idea of a girl singing in public. But over time, her voice made people forget appearances and listen with their hearts.

From the Countryside to Cairo

As she grew older, people in Cairo began hearing about her. One of those people was Sheikh Abu al-'Ila Muhammad, who encouraged her to leave the village and move to Cairo. That was a huge step in her life.

In Cairo, she met major poets and composers like Ahmed Rami, Mohamed al-Qasabgi, Zakariyya Ahmad, and later Riyad al-Sunbati. Each one of them helped her develop herself more and more, until she became known as "Kawkab al-Sharq" (Star of the East), the name people would later call her.

Fame and Her Audience

In the 1930s and 1940s, Umm Kulthum became a major star. Her concerts were broadcast on the radio, and cafés would fill up with music lovers. People would wait for the first Thursday of every month to listen to her new concert.

One thing that made her performances unique was that she would often repeat the same verse multiple times because of the audience's reaction. If the crowd said "Allah!" (a sign of deep appreciation), she'd sing the line again, stronger, or with different emotion. The relationship between Umm Kulthum and her audience was extraordinary, full of mutual love and deep understanding.

Her Songs and Language

The lyrics of Umm Kulthum's songs were always full of elegance and poetic beauty. Many were written by Ahmed Rami, who wrote over 100 songs for her. The themes of her songs touched on love, heartbreak, dignity, and even politics.

Some of her most famous songs include:

- You Are My Life
- The Ruins
- The Story of Love
- They Reminded Me
- Hope of My Life
- At Egypt's Door
- Egypt Speaks for Herself

She sometimes sang in classical Arabic (fuṣḥa), and sometimes in elegant colloquial. This made her accessible to audiences across different educational and cultural levels.

Umm Kulthum and Politics

Umm Kulthum was never far from politics. During the 1952 Revolution, she supported the Free Officers, and her songs clearly showed support for the new era. Later, her relationship with President Gamal Abdel Nasser grew strong. He, too, was a huge fan of her voice.

After the 1967 war and Egypt's defeat, Umm Kulthum began performing in Arab countries like Lebanon, Tunisia, and Morocco, raising huge amounts of money to support the Egyptian army. People didn't see her as just a singer; she was a symbol of patriotism.

Her Influence in the Arab World

No other Arab artist has had the same cultural impact as Umm Kulthum. In Morocco, they called her "El Sett" (The Lady). In Iraq, people would stay up all night to listen to her concerts. In Lebanon, her fans memorized her songs word for word.

Even after her death, her voice is still played on the radio, and new generations continue to discover her. As many say, "There are many singers, but only one Umm Kulthum."

Death and Legacy

Umm Kulthum passed away in 1975, and her funeral was one of the largest Egypt has ever seen. Millions of people filled the streets to say goodbye. To them, she wasn't just an artist; she was part of their lives, their memories, and their identity.

To this day, Umm Kulthum is still with us, in her songs, in photos, in documentaries, and in the heart of anyone who loves true, timeless Arabic music.

Magdi Yacoub

Magdi Yacoub: The Heart Doctor Loved by All

Some people go down in history because of their fame. Others leave their mark because of their impact. Magdi Yacoubis the second kind. An Egyptian heart surgeon—not just a successful doctor, but a human being who leaves a lasting mark on every heart he heals, every young person he inspires, and every poor patient he helps.

Childhood and Beginnings

Magdi Yacoub was born in 1935 in the city of Belbeis in Sharqia Governorate, into a well-educated Coptic Christian family. His father was a doctor, which had a big influence on him. As a child, he would watch his father treat patients and saw how medicine could change lives.

But the moment that truly shaped his destiny was when his aunt died suddenly from a heart condition. From that moment on, he decided to dedicate his life to studying and performing heart surgery, so that no one else would have to lose a loved one in the same way.

Studying Abroad in the UK

After graduating from the Faculty of Medicine at Cairo University, he traveled to England to specialize further. There, he faced many challenges: language barriers, homesickness, and the intense pressure of the job. But he had passion, determination, and extraordinary talent.

He worked in top hospitals, always eager to learn new things and try advanced techniques. After years of hard work, he became one of the most renowned heart surgeons in the world.

Global Achievements

One of his greatest contributions was helping develop techniques for heart transplantation. He performed extremely complex surgeries for patients who had nearly lost hope. In the 1980s, he became head of cardiac surgery at Harefield Hospital in London, where he performed the highest number of heart transplants in Europe.

He received many awards, including being knighted by Queen Elizabeth II in 1992, a major honor in the UK. But he always said that the greatest reward was a patient's smile after recovering.

Returning to Egypt and Humanitarian Work

Even though he spent most of his life in the UK, Magdi Yacoub never forgot Egypt. He always dreamed of coming back to help his country. And in 2009, he established the Magdi Yacoub Heart Center in Aswan, which provides completely free heart treatment, especially for children.

This center has become one of the best places in the Middle East for cardiac surgery and welcomes thousands of patients from Egypt and across the Arab world. It also trains doctors and nurses, and conducts cutting-edge medical research.

Humility and Humanity

Despite all his success, Magdi Yacoub is known for his deep humility. He doesn't like to talk about himself and always says that what he does is a duty, not a favor. He spends long hours in surgery and talks to patients with the compassion of a father, not just a doctor.

He believes that science should serve people, and that medicine without compassion is meaningless. That's why he's not just a physician, but also a rare and admirable human being.

A Lasting Legacy

Today, Magdi Yacoub is a symbol not just of scientific achievement, but also of kindness and giving. Many young people in Egypt and the Arab world see him as a role model and say they want to be like him.

He's living proof that you can reach global excellence, stay true to your roots, and use your knowledge to help others.

Omar Sharif

Omar Sharif: A Star from Egypt to Hollywood

Omar Sharif wasn't just a famous actor; he was a bridge between East and West, between Egypt and the world. From the moment he appeared on screen, people felt he was different. His looks, his presence, the way he spoke... all of that made him a star quickly. But what kept him in people's memory wasn't just his appearance or talent; it was also his journey, full of challenges and difficult choices.

His Childhood and Early Career in Egypt

Omar Sharif was born in 1932 in Alexandria, to a Catholic Christian family of Lebanese descent. His real name was Michel Shalhoub. From a young age, he loved acting and used to perform in school plays. Later, he enrolled at the American University in Cairo, studying math and physics, but his heart was in the arts.

His first real step into the film world came when director Youssef Chahine met him and cast him in the film Struggle in the Valley (Ṣirāʿ fī al-Wādī) in 1954, opposite Faten Hamama, who would later become his wife.

The Love of His Life: Faten Hamama

The love story between Omar Sharif and Faten Hamama was the talk of the town. Even though they were from different religions, Omar converted to Islam to marry her. They became a hugely successful artistic duo, appearing together in multiple films.

But after several years, due to Omar's travel and busy international career, they eventually separated. Still, he always said Faten was the true love of his life and that he never loved anyone else.

The Road to Hollywood

In the early 1960s, Omar was offered a role in Lawrence of Arabia, a turning point in his global career. That role brought him massive fame, earned him an Academy Award nomination, and won him a Golden Globe.

After that, he starred in several other major international films like Doctor Zhivago and Funny Girl with Barbra Streisand, and it was rumored that they had a romantic relationship.

But despite his success, Omar Sharif often felt a sense of alienation. He wasn't completely comfortable with the Hollywood lifestyle and sometimes missed his life in Egypt.

Identity and Belonging

Despite his global fame, Omar Sharif never forgot Egypt. He always spoke fondly of his country and felt like a "son of the Nile," even when living in Paris or Los Angeles. At the same time, he felt he couldn't easily return to Egypt, especially after separating from Faten, and after his life had changed so drastically.

His life was full of inner conflict: between the love of fame and the feeling of loneliness, between the West that welcomed him and the East he missed.

Final Years and Death

In his later years, Omar Sharif acted less and lived a quieter life. In 2015, he passed away from a heart attack, after suffering from Alzheimer's disease in his final months.

When he died, all of Egypt mourned him. Not just because he was a global star, but because he was a symbol of a whole generation, a generation that dreamed, loved cinema and saw in Omar Sharif the image of a successful Egyptian who reached the world stage.

His Artistic Legacy

Omar Sharif left behind a long legacy of important films, both in Egypt and abroad. He left the image of the charming Arab man in people's minds and made Egypt's name known at the biggest international film festivals.

He wasn't just an artist; he was a story of success, a story of love, a story of inner conflict. And that's why Omar Sharif will remain in memory not only as an actor, but as a symbol of a bridge between two cultures.

Safiya Zaghloul

Safiya Zaghloul: Mother of the Egyptians and Heart of the Revolution

When we talk about Egypt's national struggle, we have to mention Safiya Zaghloul. Not just because she was married to a great political leader, but because she herself was a leader, a powerful voice for freedom and independence. She was called "Umm al-Masriyyīn" (Mother of the Egyptians), and that title wasn't just a compliment; it was a reflection of the love and respect of an entire nation.

Early Life and Education

Safiya Zaghloul was born in 1876. She was the daughter of Mustafa Fahmy Pasha, who served as Prime Minister of Egypt at the time. So, she came from a high-class background and received a good education in foreign-language schools. She was raised with aristocratic customs and discipline.

Despite that, she wasn't spoiled or disconnected from reality. On the contrary, she was cultured, loved reading, and had a strong personality. In 1896, she married Saad Zaghloul, who at the time was an ambitious young man at the start of his political career.

A Partnership in Struggle, Not Just in Marriage

Her relationship with Saad wasn't just a traditional marriage. They were true partners in both thought and activism. She was always involved in the political discussions that took place in their home, which was always open to intellectuals and politicians.

When Saad began leading a nationalist movement against the British occupation, Safiya wasn't in the background; she was right at the front lines.

The 1919 Revolution and Safiya's Role

When the British exiled Saad Zaghloul to Malta in March 1919, Egypt erupted. People took to the streets in protest, and, for the first time, large numbers of women joined the demonstrations, chanting against the occupation.

Safiya Zaghloul was at the heart of it all. She organized protests, hosted women in Bayt al-Umma ("The House of the Nation"), and supported the movement with full force. Her presence inspired many women to participate, and her voice was respected and influential.

The house she lived in became known as "Bayt al-Umma," because it served as the headquarters of national activity. There, she met with citizens, coordinated efforts, wrote letters, and followed all political developments closely.

Mother of the Egyptians

After the people saw her courage and commitment, they began calling her "Mother of the Egyptians." That title wasn't given lightly. She spoke in the name of the people, defended their cause, and sacrificed her comfort and privacy for the sake of independence.

She remained in that role even after Saad returned from exile and became Prime Minister. And after his death in 1927, she didn't disappear from public life; she stayed active and continued defending his values and vision.

Her Role in Empowering Women

Safiya Zaghloul didn't just fight for the country's freedom; she also believed in the importance of women's roles in society. She believed that women should have a voice and be part of building the nation.

Her political presence encouraged many women to enter the public sphere, whether in politics, education, or social work. She was a symbol of the strong, educated woman who could be patriotic and courageous at the same time.

Her Final Years and Legacy

In her final years, she lived a quiet life but continued to follow politics and welcome visitors at Bayt al-Umma. She passed away in 1946, but her memory is still alive.

Safiya Zaghloul was a rare model of a strong, educated, patriotic woman who was respected by all. She left her mark on history and left behind a living example for future generations of what it means to be engaged, committed, and brave.

Taha Hussein

Taha Hussein: The Power of the Mind Is Greater Than Sight

If anyone deserves the title "Dean of Arabic Literature," it's Taha Hussein. Not just because he wrote important books, but because he had a wide-reaching vision to enlighten society through education and culture. He was also living proof that a disability is not the end but the beginning of an extraordinary story.

Childhood and the Loss of Sight

Taha Hussein was born in 1889 in a small village called Izbet al-Kilo in the Minya Governorate in Upper Egypt. When he was about three years old, he caught an eye infection, and due to the lack of proper medical care at the time, he lost his sight completely. But he didn't give up. He was always curious, intelligent, and loved to listen and memorize everything he heard.

His father was a modest government employee, and Taha was one of thirteen siblings. Even though life wasn't easy, he joined the village kuttab (traditional school) and memorized the entire Qur'an at a young age. That helped him a lot in strengthening his language and memory, skills that would later shape his literary style.

From Al-Azhar to France

After finishing the kuttab, he moved to Cairo and joined Al-Azhar, where he studied Islamic jurisprudence, grammar, and hadith. But over time, he began to feel that the teaching there was too rigid and didn't encourage critical thinking. When Cairo University (then called the Egyptian University) opened in 1908, he enrolled and was among its first students.

At the university, he met both Egyptian and foreign professors. His thinking expanded, and he dove deeper into literature, history, and philosophy. His doctoral thesis was about Abu al-'Alaa al-Ma'arri, and he openly stated his opinions, something that drew strong criticism from many people. But he wasn't afraid and stood firm in his belief in freedom of thought.

In 1914, he traveled to France to continue his studies. There he met Suzanne, who later became his wife. She helped him adjust to life abroad, read to him, and translated materials. He studied at the Sorbonne and earned another doctorate in literature.

Education and Reform

When he returned to Egypt, he worked as a professor at Cairo University, then became Dean of the Faculty of Arts, and later Minister of Education. During that time, he tried to transform education in Egypt.

He famously said: "Education is like water and air; it is a right for every citizen." He believed Egypt would never progress unless everyone, rich or poor, man or woman, had access to education.

He promoted girls' education and encouraged teaching literature and critical thinking, not just memorization and rote learning. He always aimed to make the university a space for free research and open discussion, not just a factory for degrees.

His Books and Ideas

Taha Hussein wrote many important works. Some of his most well-known books include:

- The Days: an autobiographical account of his childhood and life
- On Pre-Islamic Poetry: a controversial book that sparked major debate
- The Future of Culture in Egypt: a book about education and national development
- Wednesday Conversations: essays on literature and criticism

His ideas always revolved around rationalism, freedom, and the right to question and think. He believed literature was not just beautiful words; it was a way to understand oneself and society.

Challenges and Backlash

Because of his bold ideas, Taha Hussein faced intense criticism from religious leaders, politicians, and even fellow intellectuals. Some insulted him, others tried to ban his books.

But he remained true to his principles, always responding with reason and logic. He didn't like confrontation, but he also refused to stay silent in the face of ignorance or fanaticism.

Despite the attacks, he became one of the most influential thinkers who reshaped how people thought in the Arab world.

His Final Years and Legacy

Taha Hussein kept writing until the very end of his life, despite aging and physical weakness. He passed away in 1973, but to this day, his name still shines in every conversation about education, culture, or intellectual freedom.

He wasn't just a writer or minister; he was a living dream: the dream that any child from a small village can reach university, even if he can't see.

Taha Hussein is living proof that the mind is stronger than any disability, and that words can change an entire society.

Omar Khairat

Omar Khairat: Music That Speaks Without Words

The moment you hear one of his melodies, you feel like you've entered a different world. Omar Khairat has crafted a musical style that blends refined emotion with an unmistakably Egyptian spirit. Without a single lyric, he expresses feelings and stories, touching listeners through a single note or powerful phrase. His music has become part of the Egyptian ear and a soundtrack to many people's lives.

Beginnings: A Home Full of Music

Omar Khairat was born in 1948, into a musical family in the Sayyida Zeinab neighborhood of Cairo. His grandfather, Mahmoud Khairat, was a well-known musician and composer, and his brother was also a pianist.

From an early age, music surrounded him, so it was only natural that he would follow that path. He began learning piano as a child, then studied at the Cairo Conservatory, focusing on Western classical music.

But despite his classical training, he always had a passion for infusing his music with Egyptian feeling and identity.

From Band Member to Star

As a young man, he was a member of a musical group called Les Petits Chats, one of the most popular Western-style bands in Egypt during the 1960s. This experience introduced him to a wide audience and brought him closer to everyday people.

Later, he shifted toward composing music for theater and film. This marked a new chapter in his life, one that connected his name to the emotional memory of Egyptian audiences.

His Music: Stories Without Words

What makes Omar Khairat's music stand out is how it tells stories without any lyrics. You can hear a melody and feel sadness, joy, nostalgia, or even suspense. He knows how to use instruments to paint a full emotional picture.

In his work, you can hear influences from jazz, classical, and traditional Arabic music. He blends them in a way that's entirely his own.

Many people don't typically enjoy instrumental music. But when they hear Omar Khairat, they often feel like they've understood a story without anyone saying a word.

Famous Works That Made Him a Cultural Icon

Some of his best-known pieces include:

- The Conscience of Abla Hekmat (TV)
- Face of the Moon
- The Return of the Stranger
- The Search for Sayyid Marzouk (Film)
- The Second Encounter

- New arrangements of songs by Umm Kulthum and Abdel Halim Hafez

These pieces are unforgettable. His concerts are always sold out. People of all ages come to listen, and many know his melodies by heart, just like they would a popular song.

His Concerts: An Experience Like No Other

Omar Khairat's concerts aren't just musical events; they're full experiences. The stage is lit, the audience is silent, and every note touches something deep inside.

Many say they leave his concerts emotionally moved, as if they had lived through a dream or a film. This shows just how deeply his music resonates with people.

Inspiration and Education

Omar Khairat isn't just a performer; he's also a source of inspiration for young musicians. Many music students in Egypt and the Arab world see him as a role model.

He also played a big part in elevating instrumental music in the Arab world, making it accessible to people who had never listened to non-vocal music before.

Ongoing Connection with the Public

Despite the passing years, Omar Khairat continues to hold a special place in people's hearts. Every concert he gives trends online, and any new project creates excitement.

People love him not just for his music, but for his humility, respect for his audience, and tireless dedication to his craft.

Podcasts

Naguib Mahfouz

- Welcome to you. Today we're going to talk about a really big name that all of us know: Naguib Mahfouz.

- Welcome. And who doesn't know Naguib Mahfouz, of course.

- But maybe the question we want to stop at a little: why do we consider him more than just a skillful novelist? What does the idea mean, that he's a social historian?

- Alright, look, the word mu'arrikh ijtima'i is very important. It's not just a title and that's it. No, it describes Mahfouz's own work. He wasn't writing history in the traditional sense—like battles and sultans and so on. No, he was documenting Egyptian society, analyzing it, seeing the changes happening in it, the people, the details of their daily lives.

- Meaning, like he was photographing Egypt from the inside.

- Exactly. It's like he had a camera and went into Egypt's old houses, its streets, its alleyways. He saw so many things and managed to express them. Even the coffeehouses—the places where people sit and talk and drink tea and coffee—he portrayed them as a very important space for social life, and also intellectual life.

- And that of course has a connection with his upbringing in Gamaliya in 1911. Do you think that environment, old Cairo with all its details, is what shaped his awareness, his understanding of Egyptian life?

- For sure, of course. A person is influenced by the place he grows up in— especially an artist sensitive like Mahfouz. Gamaliya, yes, it planted in him a very deep understanding of people and Egyptian life. And add to that his love of reading from when he was very young, and then his study of philosophy. All of this sharpened his outlook on things. It was clear that inside him there was a true love for literature and for thought from long ago—a real passion.

- Okay, and he started his practical life as an ordinary government employee. What made him focus on writing to that extent? And why did he leave Pharaonic history, which he started with, and focus more on the Egyptian reality we live in?

- He started first with historical novels like Kifah Tiba (The Struggle of Thebes) and Radobis. Maybe that was a search for identity, for ancient Egyptian roots. But then came the big transformation, and he turned his lens toward the reality he was living. He focused in particular on the life of the middle class, which is, I mean, that big segment of people who aren't very rich and aren't very poor.

- Like he found that this was the space where he could really express Egypt.

- Exactly. Maybe he felt, sensed, that this was his field, where he could talk about questions of existence, society, and the contemporary Egyptian person.

- And here we must talk about the Thulathiyya (The Trilogy)—Bayn al-Qasrayn, Qasr al-Shawq, al-Sukkariyya. People call it an epic. How does this Trilogy show the idea of the "social historian" we mentioned?

- The Trilogy is a really excellent example. On the surface, it's the story of a family—the family of Sayyid Ahmad Abd al-Jawad. But through this family we see the whole history of Egypt changing before us, generation after generation. The father himself, the one we call "strict"—I mean, very harsh and firm in his house with his children.

- Yes, that famous character.

- Right. He's not just an authoritarian father, and that's it. He represented the values of an entire patriarchal society. He was facing the challenges of modernity and changing ideas with his children. Mahfouz used this family like a miniature Egypt. We see in it all the transformations that happened in the country in a very important period.

- Mmm, I see what you mean. Okay, and another thing that really distinguishes Mahfouz: his writing style. The thing people call 'simple but profound.' What does that mean exactly?

- This is Mahfouz's genius in language, really. He didn't like to show off with difficult, complicated language. He used clear language, close to the people's language, the way we speak.

- But not superficial, right?

- No, no, not at all. This is the idea of 'simple but profound.' You read the sentence easily, but to understand everything behind it—the deep philosophical, psychological, and social meanings—you have to stop and think a little. And in addition, of course, his descriptions of places, that's a whole story in itself. He makes you feel like you're walking in the street he's describing.

- But not all his works passed without problems. 'Children of the Alley' in particular—we heard it made huge problems, even to the point that there was an attempt for it to be banned.

- Yes. 'Children of the Alley' was a very symbolic and complex novel. It talked about sensitive topics like the relationship between religion, science, and power across history. Some people at the time interpreted those symbols in a way they considered offensive to religions. And that's what caused the big attack on it and the attempts to ban it.

- Meaning, he was bold in his ideas, even if he knew they might cause him problems.

- Exactly. And this shows us that he wasn't afraid to raise the big, important questions.

- And despite all that attack, and even the assassination attempt that happened to him and affected him physically, we hear that Mahfouz was a person who avoided confrontation—he wasn't someone for direct fights and conflicts.

- That's true, a very important point. He expressed all these bold ideas in his writings and in his art. But in his personal life, he was calm and peaceful. He avoided sharp confrontations and verbal battles.

- Maybe that was wisdom from him.

- Very possible. Maybe that's what allowed him to keep going and write all that great body of work. And then his Nobel Prize in 1988—that was a really huge international recognition for him and for Arabic literature as a whole, of course.

- And what's striking is that even after Nobel he stayed the same—simple and calm in his life.

- Naguib Mahfouz passed away in 2006. But he left behind for us, as we say, a huge legacy, a really big heritage.

- Exactly. A legacy not just in the number of books, but in the value itself—the artistic and intellectual value in his works. That's why reading Naguib Mahfouz until today is not just literary enjoyment. It's, I mean, a necessity if we want to understand Egypt, to understand its spirit, its history, its transformations in the twentieth century. He really was a living record of the memory of a whole nation. And that makes us think of a question at the end: how can one writer manage to do all that—to document and summarize an entire society with its history and its complexities inside novels and stories? What are the tools that a writer must have to be able to do that? A question worth thinking about.

o   A really important question.

Yousra

o   Welcome everyone. Today we're going to take a closer look at a very engaging article. Its subject is an artist who holds a very special place for all of us—the actress Yousra. We'll try to understand her journey and her impact, as the article presents them. There's a lovely expression in the article: "many faces but one heart." This phrase nicely sums up the idea of variety in her roles. She has played a huge range of parts over more than forty years, yet always with one consistent spirit and essence. The article tells us her real name is Seveen Hafez Naseem, and that her career began in the late 1970s—small roles at first, but she quickly drew attention. The key point the article emphasizes is that she didn't just rely on her looks. She worked hard on herself and developed her talent.

o   Exactly. And here the article points to a very important turning point: her collaboration with the great director Youssef Shahin. Their work together in films like 'An Egyptian Story' and 'Alexandria Again and Forever' presented Yousra in a completely different light. She was no longer just the pretty star—she became an actress of depth and thought. The article explains that this showed her as a serious actress capable of handling difficult and complex roles.

o   True. And what about the next stage? The article shifts to her work with Adel Imam. Is there a link there?

o   The article sees her work with Adel Imam as a very different kind of success. It describes them as a highly successful duo. The term here, as the article explains, means a complete artistic pair on screen, with amazing chemistry between them. The examples are numerous: 'The Human and the Jinn,' 'A Squatter in the Street,' and 'Terrorism and Kebab'—all unforgettable films.

o   Yes, films we all remember very well.

o   And the article uses another nice expression—'real chemistry.' This means the natural harmony and attraction between them was real and came through on screen, which is why audiences always loved seeing them together.

o   Right. From cinema, the article then moves to television and says her success there was also huge.

o   Of course. The article uses a beautiful phrase, saying her TV dramas 'touched people.' That means her work resonated with ordinary people—their feelings, their lives, their problems, and experiences.

- Like what, for example? Does the article mention examples?

- Yes, it mentions 'Where is My Heart?"), 'A Public Opinion Case,' among others. What really stands out in her TV work, as the article hints, is her ability to convey emotions with simplicity and honesty. Whether playing the role of a mother, a wife, or even a judge, she always came across as genuine. The performance reached the audience immediately.

- And the article doesn't just focus on Yousra the artist. It also talks about Yousra the person. It mentions her involvement in charity initiatives, her support for important causes like women's issues and cancer awareness, and also her role as a Goodwill Ambassador for the United Nations.

- The article explains that this role means she used her fame to serve bigger humanitarian and social causes. That's very important, and it connects with the overall picture the article paints of her—as a model of the modern Egyptian woman. It presents her as an example of a strong and successful woman who managed to achieve herself, meaning to fulfill her ambitions and prove herself in a tough field like art.

- Exactly.

- The article also emphasizes that she has always been careful to preserve her reputation and the respect of the public. That's why, in the end, it describes her as an icon.

- An icon!

- Yes, an icon not only in art, but also in elegance and fashion. The word īqūna here gives the sense of a symbol or role model—someone you look up to and learn from.

- Another point in the article is the continuity of her popularity generation after generation. This means not only the audience who saw her early work still loves her, but also the younger generations continue to follow and admire her. That shows how capable she is of renewing herself, working with younger artists, and staying up to date.

- Exactly. And that's why, in the end, as the article says, she has become part of Egypt's and the Arab world's artistic memory. Her connection with the audience is strong and ongoing—and that, in itself, is something remarkable and worthy of study.

- So, this article managed to present us with a full picture of Yousra: her talent, her range, her determination and hard work, her important humanitarian side, and her extraordinary ability to last and succeed for so many years.

- And in the end, the article leaves us with an implicit question: what's the secret? How did an artist like Yousra manage to keep her star power, her respect, and her influence for so long? How did she remain so firmly in our artistic and cultural consciousness, in a field that changes as fast as lightning? A very important question indeed.

Rifa'a al-Tahtawi

- Welcome to you. Today we're going to talk about a very important article that deals with a truly pivotal figure in Egypt's modern history: Rifa'a al-Tahtawi. This article presents him as a pioneer of the Egyptian renaissance in the 19th century, and it tries to explain to us how his ideas contributed to shaping the Egypt we know.

- Welcome. And it really is a special article because it presents al-Tahtawi not just as a religious scholar or a translator, no not at all. It considers him the owner of a big intellectual project. And the article makes clear that the goal of this project was finding that difficult balance between authenticity and renewal.

- Authenticity and renewal...

- Exactly. Meaning, how to take from what is new and benefit from it, and at the same time preserve our identity and our Egyptian character. That was basically his main equation.

- Okay, let's start from the beginning, like the article does. It tells about his upbringing in Tahta in Upper Egypt, and then his studies at al-Azhar. And from that time, he had a curiosity that was a bit different—not just memorization and that's it, but he wanted to understand deeply. Exactly. And we can say this was the first seed of his critical thinking, which developed later. And the article links this directly to his journey to France, which was a completely different turning point in his life.

- Yes, that France point is very important, and the article gives it a big space. In 1826, he traveled with the first educational mission in the era of Muhammad 'Ali. But the strange thing is that he wasn't going at first as a student.

- No, not at all. He went as the imam of the mission, meaning his role was religious and guiding for the students who were going to study. But his being there in the heart of Paris opened his eyes to a completely different world.

- How so?

- The article considers that journey a real turning point in his thinking. It even uses the expression ' cultural shock'—but in a positive sense. He saw a different education system, administrative organization, concern for law, modern sciences. The article says he was amazed by all of this.

o   And he came back then with a completely new vision for Egypt.

o   Exactly. And when he returned, the article really emphasizes this point: he didn't settle for just translating books, and that's it.

o   No? How so?

o   He was trying to transfer the ideas and concepts behind those texts. And of course he worked at the School of Languages, which the article considers a center of radiance at that time. And he had a very strong concern with simplifying these concepts.

o   What does "simplifying the concepts" mean?

o   The article says that he tried to find suitable Arabic words for new terms, or explain them with examples from Egyptian daily life so that ordinary people could understand them and absorb them.

o   And all this came from his belief in education, right?

o   Of course. The article makes clear that education was the cornerstone of his renaissance project. Not just any education, but comprehensive and accessible education. That's why we find the article highlighting his efforts in developing curricula and establishing new schools.

o   And even girls' education.

o   Of course, because that was a very forward-thinking idea for his time, and really it was a very bold step in Egyptian society back then.

o   Okay, and what about the bigger project, which was benefiting from the West? How does the article present that?

o   The article explains that he wanted to take the useful things from Western civilization, especially in sciences and administration, but he always had a warning against blind imitation. Meaning, not to take everything as it is, but to take what suits us and fits with our values and our religion. He saw that science and religion could go together.

o   And despite all this, the article says he faced difficulties and challenges.

o   Of course there were, naturally—resistance from conservative currents, and sometimes political changes that affected his roles and positions. But the article stresses his commitment to his principles and his insistence on this intellectual project.

o   And because of that, his influence continued.

o Exactly. The article concludes by considering him a role model and an inspiration for many generations that came after him. And his ideas about education, about women, about the relationship between religion and science—these are things we are still discussing until today.

o So we can summarize and say that this article draws for us a picture of Rifa'a al-Tahtawi as a key figure who opened the door to modernization in Egypt, and who used conscious translation and education as basic tools to build bridges between cultures while preserving identity.

o Exactly. He of course didn't do everything by himself, but he started the path and laid down very important foundations. And the article leaves us at the end with an important question to think about: this experience of al-Tahtawi makes us always ask ourselves—how do we achieve the progress we want without losing our identity? And is his equation of asala wa tajdid still relevant or inspiring in today's fast world? That's really an open question.

Gamal Abdel Nasser

o Welcome to you. Today we're going to talk about a very important personality in Egypt's modern history: Gamal Abdel Nasser. We'll look together at the story of his life and the big events that were connected with him. He's someone who was born at a time when Egypt was still suffering from occupation, and who saw with his own eyes injustice and inequality—and that, most likely, was the driving force behind his long journey for change.

o Exactly. And those circumstances really shaped his political awareness from when he was still young. And these ideas grew with him, step by step, until he led one of the most important transformations in the history of Egypt and the entire region. Let's start this journey together.

o Alright. Abdel Nasser was born in 1918, and his childhood was spent moving between many places because of his father's work. That may have allowed him to see different parts of society. And more importantly, from early on, while still young, he was interested in politics, taking part in demonstrations and reading about independence. I mean, there was an early awareness.

o Yes. And this interest continued with him. It wasn't just, I mean, youthful enthusiasm and that's it. When he entered the military academy in 1937, the matter took another form. There, he began to meet officers who had the same thinking, the same dream of changing the country. These were the ones who later became known as the Free Officers. Here, the idea started to turn into a real organization.

o And of course the conditions at that time, I mean, helped with that. There was corruption, a wide gap between social classes, and still foreign influence and control. All of that led to the night of 23 July 1952—the night when Abdel Nasser and the Free Officers decided to move, took control of key centers in the country, and forced King Farouk to abdicate the throne. That was truly a decisive turning point.

o Correct. And in the beginning, the leadership wasn't Abdel Nasser's alone. There were other names, like Mohamed Naguib, for example. But with time, the very dynamics of power and the developments that took place made Abdel Nasser emerge as the actual leader of the movement. And this was confirmed officially when he was elected President of Egypt in 1956.

o And here we arrive at one of the most important stations in his history and in all of modern Egyptian history: the nationalization of the Suez Canal. That was on 26 July 1956. Abdel Nasser announced that decision in a very famous speech in Alexandria. The decision came as a direct response to the refusal of the World Bank and Western powers to finance the High Dam project. And the term ta'mim here, as we see, simply means that the canal became the property of the Egyptian state, under its management and sovereignty.

o Exactly. And that decision, of course, didn't pass quietly. The international reaction was very violent. There was the military attack known as the Tripartite Aggression—by whom? Britain, France, and Israel. But what is really striking is the steadfastness of the Egyptian people at that time. The word 'samad' (to stand firm) has a very strong meaning here: steadfastness and resistance despite all pressures. And in the end, because of international pressure and popular resistance, the invading forces were forced to withdraw. And more important than the immediate military result was that this ta'mim entrenched and raised very highly the concept national dignity. And not just in Egypt—its echo reached the whole Arab world, and even other countries in the developing world.

o Correct. And that ta'mim opened the door to a bigger idea that Abdel Nasser had: the idea of Arab unity. He had a big dream of Arab nationalism. And there was indeed an attempt to realize this dream when Egypt and Syria united in 1958 and formed the United Arab Republic.

o Exactly. That experiment maybe didn't last very long—they separated after a few years—but the idea itself, the idea of Arab nationalism, remained strong and very influential in the region. Abdel Nasser connected this nationalism with basic issues like the liberation of Palestine, confronting colonialism, and achieving a kind of Arab economic integration. And his ability to address Arab masses with speeches that were simple, direct, and powerful was one of the reasons for his huge popularity throughout the Arab world.

o   But this journey faced a very difficult challenge, even a huge shock, in 1967—that was the June War, which became known in the media and among the people as the Naksa (the Setback). The military defeat was harsh, and it led to the occupation of important parts of Arab land—first of all Sinai, of course, as well as the Golan and the West Bank.

o   It was a shock in every sense, to the extent that Abdel Nasser himself came out and announced that he would step down. The word 'step down' here means that he decided to leave power, to resign. But what happened was astonishing: millions went down to the streets in Egypt and in other Arab capitals, demanding that he stay in power, rejecting his resignation. So he really did return, and began a new and different stage: rebuilding the armed forces, and starting what became known as the War of Attrition on the Suez Canal front. It was a stage of preparation and readiness for the coming battles to regain the land.

o   But unfortunately, fate had another opinion. This journey ended suddenly and shockingly on 28 September 1970. Gamal Abdel Nasser died suddenly of a heart attack. He was only 52 years old. The news of his death was an enormous shock in Egypt and throughout the Arab world.

o   Indeed. And as we always see until today, opinions differ about evaluating Abdel Nasser's period of rule and his legacy. Some people see him as a historic national leader who achieved accomplishments like the ta'mim and the High Dam, and who raised the pride of Egypt and the Arabs. And other people criticize aspects of his domestic and foreign policies, or talk about the effects of his rule on political and economic life. But what there is no doubt about is that he was a figure who changed the face of Egypt and the region in a major way, and who entrenched key concepts like national dignity and social justice as essential popular demands. People still talk about the days of Abdel Nasser, or 'the era of Abdel Nasser,' whether positively or negatively.

o   Exactly. So with that, we've taken a quick but important look at the career of Gamal Abdel Nasser—from his beginnings and being shaped by the circumstances around him, to leading the revolution, to his historic decisions like the ta'mim, to his dream of Arab nationalism, and also the huge challenges he faced like the naksa and his steadfastness afterward until his sudden death.

o   And the question always remains open for thought and discussion: how can a personality with all these complexities—with all its positives and negatives—remain influential and present in the collective memory of peoples after all these years? And are there specific lessons we can draw from an experience like this, in the peoples' continuous pursuit of dignity and independence in our contemporary world? I think that's an important question, one that needs reflection.

Rania Al-Mashat

- o Today we're going to talk about a personality who has recently appeared strongly on the Egyptian scene: Rania Al-Mashat. She's known for having a strong presence, I mean clear charisma, influence, and self-confidence that always shows.

- o True. And she's an important model of the Egyptian woman who managed to reach leadership and important positions, representing her country in international forums. Let's review her journey and the most important stations in it.

- o The beginning was, I mean, very strong education—economics at the American University here in Cairo, and then a master's and doctorate from the University of Maryland in the US.

- o Mmm.

- o And what's striking is that her academic focus was on macroeconomics and monetary policies.

- o That term—monetary policies—what does it refer to exactly?

- o Look, monetary policies, simply, are the tools and procedures that the Central Bank uses to control the money supply in the country—the liquidity, the interest rate—and thus affect the economy as a whole.

- o Alright. And this study, it prepared her for what later in her work?

- o It prepared her directly. She started at the Central Bank of Egypt, and then—an important step—she went to Washington and worked at the IMF.

- o Yes, the IMF exactly. And of course that fund is a major international institution that provides assistance and economic advice to countries. But more important than just the work itself was the type of experience she gained.

- o Like what, for example?

- o I mean, she participated in negotiations—those are discussions and talks to reach agreements with different countries. And she also contributed to designing economic reform programs.

- Economic reform programs—those are plans that change or try to improve a certain country's economy?

- Exactly. Comprehensive plans. And that experience—specifically dealing directly with crises and designing practical solutions—that's what shaped a big part of her ability later to manage complex files.

- Now we come to a very important turning point: her becoming Minister of Tourism in 2018. At that time, the tourism sector was facing major challenges, right?

- Yes, it was really a tough time. But she came in with a slightly different approach. She focused strongly on presenting Egypt with a modern image.

- A modern image. What does that mean?

- It means a modern, attractive, globally up-to-date look. Not just relying on the historic and archaeological image, but also showing the modern face of Egypt. And this was an important strategic shift at that time.

- Like the campaigns she did—"People to People" and so on?

- Yes, campaigns like "People to People" and "Experience Egypt." She used social media and human stories in a very innovative way to deliver a different, fresh message about Egypt.

- Mmm. Okay, was that focus just marketing, like just publicity?

- No, it wasn't just marketing. It was part of a broader vision. There was clear attention to training people working in the tourism sector itself, raising the quality of services, and improving the tourist's overall experience.

- And the result?

- The result was the beginning of a gradual recovery in tourism. And that's considered a big success given the tough circumstances at the time.

- Alright. And then in 2020 she moved to a completely different position— Minister of International Cooperation. That's a position totally different from tourism.

- Completely different. This position requires a special mix of diplomacy, deep economic understanding, and high negotiation skills—which she had already gained earlier.

- And what was her main task in that ministry?

- Her main task was coordinating Egypt's relations with international institutions and development partners. We're talking about institutions like the World Bank, the United Nations, the European Union, and many others.

- o The striking point here, and one that often repeats in her statements, is linking those funds to specific goals.

- o True. That's a central point in her work: linking international financing to sustainable development). This term is important to understand well.

- o Which means what exactly—sustainable development?

- o Sustainable development means that the money coming from abroad—the financing—has to go to projects with long-term positive impact. Projects that serve the present generation, and at the same time don't harm the ability of future generations to meet their needs.

- o Like schools and clean energy projects and so on?

- o Exactly. Education, health, renewable energy, infrastructure that really and sustainably improves people's lives—not just temporary projects.

- o And to organize this work between the government and these international entities, she created a mechanism, right?

- o Yes. She launched something called the Joint Coordinated Cooperation Platform. The idea was simply to make dialogue and coordination easier between all the government bodies on one side, and international partners on the other.

- o So that everyone can see the full picture?

- o Exactly. So that everyone's on the same page, projects are implemented more efficiently, and there was a very strong focus on transparency.

- o Transparency... meaning clarity and sharing information?

- o Exactly—clarity, publishing information about where those funds are going, what those projects are doing. And of course that increases trust and helps accountability.

- o And that definitely affected her international image.

- o Of course. She represented Egypt in many major international forums. And the international media always highlighted her as a modern Egyptian face—a leader capable of handling complex economic and political files with high competence.

- o That's besides her personal style—her way of appearing and speaking.

- o Yes. There's always talk about the elegance of her dress and her organized, clear way of speaking—where she often relies on numbers and facts. And also her activity on social media, which was noticeable in showing the ministry's work and communicating.

- o So we can say she presented a different model for a minister or government official.

- o Exactly. A model that combines strong scientific expertise, practical international experience, and smart media presence. And many consider her a source of inspiration—not just for women but for leadership in general.

- o Truly, a very remarkable and striking journey—from academic excellence to experience in major international institutions, and then to these important ministerial positions in Egypt.

- o Exactly. And in the end, maybe the question that stays with us is: what could be the long-term impact of this leadership model—one that focuses strongly on transparency and linking everything to sustainable development? What impact might that have on achieving Egypt's bigger goals in the future? That's really an important question for reflection.

Mohamed Salah

- o Welcome to you. Today we're going to look carefully at a story we all know and love, but this time through a written text: the story of Mohamed Salah. The text presents it not just as the story of a successful soccer player and that's it—no.

- o No, not at all.

- o It sees it as an inspiring journey. I mean, a young man who started from a simple village and became a real source of inspiration for many people. How this journey has lessons much bigger than just sports.

- o True. And the point that really stands out in how the text presents the story is that it wasn't just about talent that God gave him and that's it—no.

- o Exactly.

- o The text focuses strongly on the idea of determination, hard work, and overcoming difficulties. The message it wants to deliver is that this success is the result of effort, work, and struggle—not just luck or coincidence.

- o And the beginning, as the story in the text says, was in Nagrig in Gharbiya. A very simple life, but it's clear the ambition was big from early on.

- o Mmm.

- o The text describes a very important detail—the hardship of the daily trips: traveling for hours every day from his village to Cairo for training with Al Mokawloon (the Contractors' Club), and then going back again at the end of the day. That alone, honestly, needed extraordinary patience and determination.

- o And that detail in particular shows us the foundation on which everything later was built. The text says that this kind of struggle and hardship is what builds the strong character that can face what comes next.

- o Right.

- o And that determination really became very clear later when the challenges grew.

- o Like when he traveled to Switzerland in 2012 to join FC Basel. Here the text hints at a completely different kind of challenge: ghurba (being away from one's home), a new language, a completely different culture.

- o Yes.

- o And then, of course, the Chelsea stage, where we all know he didn't get his full chance. Does the text explain why that period was especially difficult for him?

- o The text doesn't go much into technical or administrative details, but it focuses on Salah's own reaction. It portrays that period as if it was a push for him to prove himself even more.

- o Ah, so it was an additional challenge.

- o Exactly. And the loan period in Italy—with Fiorentina and then Roma— the text presents it as if it was a calculated step from him. An opportunity that he seized wisely to show people who he was, and to come back into the spotlight strongly.

- o Until we reached the move that really changed everything: Liverpool in 2017. And there he exploded and became one of the most important players in the world. But what's very striking is that the text strongly focuses on the idea of him "working on himself." Does that just mean physical and technical training?

- o No. I think the text hints that it's much deeper than that. Not just commitment in training. No—it's a whole lifestyle: food, sleep, mental focus, very high discipline in every detail.

- o Mmm, a lifestyle, you mean.

- o Yes.

- And maybe that's what explains the secret of his consistency at a high level for so many years. And the text also links this with his personality, which is always described as modest and humble. And that also has a big role in people's love for him, even outside the pitch.

- For sure, for sure. And with that, he became a true role model for young people—not just in Egypt, no, but his influence reached the whole Arab world, and maybe even beyond.

- Really.

- The text describes Egypt's qualification for the 2018 World Cup as a historic, defining moment, and how Salah was at the heart of that joy. And it also reminds us of his connection to his roots and his village, and his ongoing support for his hometown and for charitable projects. And this serves the bigger idea that the text is trying to convey: that Salah went beyond being just a successful soccer player, and became a public personality with great social and humanitarian influence. And that's the secret behind the great respect he receives, even from people who may not follow soccer at all.

- So, in summary, what we understand from this article is that Salah's story presents a real model of ambition and perseverance, and that modest or simple beginnings are never a barrier in front of big dreams, as long as there is determination and real effort. And as we always say—the story is still continuing.

- Exactly. And one last point we can think about after reading the story this way through the text: if we remove soccer completely from the equation, what's the main lesson that anyone could take from an experience like this and apply in his own life while he's pursuing a goal?

- Mmm, an important question.

- Meaning, how the idea of determination and learning from difficulties and challenges, as the text portrays it, could itself be the key to any success in any field. What can we extract for our personal lives, away from the achievements on the pitch?

Umm Kulthum

- Welcome to you. Today we're diving into the story of an exceptional personality, really an icon: Umm Kulthum. A voice—if we say it's the voice of Egypt, I think everyone will agree.

- Truly, there's no disagreement on that. Her journey is amazing in every sense.

- Today we'll try to look at that journey from very simple beginnings until she became the name we all know, Star of the East.

- The beginning itself is a story on its own—from a small village in Daqahliya, Tammay al-Zahayra.

- Yes, that village is famous because of her of course.

- Exactly. And the information about her says that she started as a child memorizing Qur'an and singing in religious festivals and weddings.

- But the strange thing is the disguise story, isn't that right?

- Exactly. Because traditions at the time were strict, she dressed like boys so that her family would accept her singing in front of people.

- Wow. Imagine—such a big challenge at the very beginning. And then came the decisive move: Cairo.

- Yes. Cairo was a completely different stage in her life and career.

- A whole new world.

- Exactly. And there she began to meet the people who would make that history with her. I mean, it wasn't just her voice that made Umm Kulthum.

- You mean the poets and composers.

- Of course. Names like Ahmad Rami, Mohamed al-Qasabgi, the great Zakariya Ahmad, and Riyad al-Sunbati. These weren't just names—they shaped her artistic soul and helped her find her very unique, special voice.

- And in a relatively short time—if we look at the 1930s and 40s—she had already become Egypt's number one star.

- Undisputed. Her monthly concerts that were broadcast on the radio were, I mean, a national event—the whole country would stop for them.

- They say the streets would empty, and people were either in their homes or in the coffeehouses listening. The coffeehouses would be...

- Would be full of the connoisseurs. This word is very important in Umm Kulthum's story.

- Yes, the connoisseurs. Who exactly were they?

- They weren't just any listeners. They were people who truly understood music—musical modes, vocal performance. An audience of instinctive critics.

- So the audience had real weight.

- o Absolutely. They were an essential part of the success of those legendary concerts. Their reactions would ignite the performance.

- o And this brings us to a very important point: the interaction of the audience. It wasn't just applause and that's it.

- o Of course not. It was a live dialogue between her and the hall—a completely unique state.

- o How so?

- o For example, she might repeat a certain passage of the song—the verse/refrain—more than once, twice, three times.

- o Based on the audience's requests?

- o Not direct requests, but according to their enthusiasm and responses. When you'd hear the words 'Allah!' or 'Great!' or 'Again!' shouted strongly in the hall, she would respond and repeat. This created, like, an almost spiritual relationship between her and her listeners.

- o A very special state indeed. Okay, and the songs themselves—the lyrics she sang.

- o Those songs were another world. The words had unusual strength and poetry—artistic beauty and deep feeling.

- o She managed to sing about almost everything—love in its different forms, the pain of separation...

- o Yes, the moment of distance, she expressed it with extraordinary skill. And also about dignity, pride, and even patriotism.

- o Of course, her patriotic songs are very well known and played their role.

- o What was also special in her language was that it was a very smart mix between classical Arabic and colloquial Arabic.

- o Yes, but not just any colloquial—a colloquial we could call refined, full of respect and taste. That made her close to everyone—the intellectual and the ordinary person—all over the Arab world.

- o And that brings us to talk about her role that went beyond art, right? She had other roles too.

- o Of course. Her political and social role was clear and important. For example, her relationship with Gamal Abdel Nasser after the 1952-Revolution) was strong and well known.

- o And especially after '67.

- Exactly. After the defeat of June '67—or as it became known, the Naksa (the Setback)—Umm Kulthum here took a truly great national stance.

- What did she do exactly?

- She began doing concert tours in many Arab countries, and even went to Paris. All the proceeds from these concerts went to support the Egyptian army and the war effort.

- Wow. Meaning she used her art and her voice to serve her country's cause at a very difficult time.

- Exactly. Here she wasn't just a singer—she was a symbol of Egypt, the voice of Egypt that united and helped in times of hardship.

- And this maybe explains why her status was much greater than just a famous singer. The whole Arab world considered her "the Lady."

- Truly. That title, the Lady, has real weight and meaning. Her concerts in any Arab country were a national event there too.

- And when she died in 1975, the scene was very hard.

- Yes. Her funeral, I mean, the farewell and burial ceremony, was something extraordinary. Some say it was one of the largest popular funerals in modern history.

- Millions went out to say goodbye.

- Millions, truly. And that alone is proof of the size of her influence and how much she was part of people's lives, their emotions, and their collective memory.

- And until today her voice is still alive with us, and new generations are discovering her and loving her. There's a saying that's always repeated:

- There are many singers, but there is only one Umm Kulthum.

- Exactly. And there's a lot of truth in that.

- And this maybe makes us ask ourselves a question at the end: how could one voice, one artist, reach all of that status—not just artistically, but as part of the identity of a whole nation? What is the secret that makes art connect so deeply with the national and cultural soul of peoples across generations? A question worth thinking about.

Magdi Yacoub

- Welcome everyone. Today we're going to dive into the details of a very important article—an article about a truly exceptional figure who managed to leave a real mark not only in Egypt but worldwide. We're talking, of course, about Dr. Magdi Yacoub.

o   Exactly. And this article presents him as something very special—not just a brilliant surgeon who reached global recognition, but a rare combination of extraordinary scientific achievement and deep humanity and compassion. The article tries to show us how these came together. So, where does it begin? It starts right from his childhood, in Belbeis, Sharqiyya Governorate, in 1935. The article links his interest in medicine to the fact that he grew up in the house of a doctor—his father.

o   Yes, but there's a pivotal moment the article really emphasizes.

o   Which is?

o   The death of his aunt, when he was still a small child, due to a heart condition. The article presents this moment as the spark that lit something inside him—pushing him not only to say "I'll study medicine," but also to decide, very specifically, to specialize in heart surgery. As if he made a vow to himself to confront that illness.

o   That's very moving—the motivation. So after his studies in Egypt, the article takes us to the next big stage: traveling to England in the 1960s.

o   Right. And here the article doesn't just say he traveled and that's it—it pauses at the challenges he faced there.

o   And that's a very important point. The article doesn't paint success as something easy. It speaks honestly about the hardships of being abroad—being alone in a different country, the language challenge at first (English of course), and the heavy workload and intense training.

o   Definitely, a completely different system.

o   A different system, a different culture. But what stands out in the article is that these difficulties didn't stop him—on the contrary, they became part of shaping his strong personality and determination. The passion inside him was much stronger. And that's what led to the great achievements the whole world knows him for. The article highlights his major role in developing modern techniques for heart and lung transplants. He wasn't just performing operations—

o   He was innovating and developing them.

o   Exactly. And it mentions how he performed surgeries that were extremely complex—procedures that represented the last hope for patients who had almost given up completely.

- The article also covers his rise to very high positions, such as becoming head of the Department of Cardiothoracic Surgery at Harefield Hospital in London—one of the world's leading institutions in this field.

- And of course the title of Sir that he received from the Queen of Britain.

- Yes, and that's considered the highest civilian honor in the UK—a recognition of his contributions to science and to people's lives.

- But the most beautiful part, the part the article focuses on strongly, is his own famous comment.

- Yes, that the most important honor isn't all those titles.

- Exactly. The most important honor, he says, is seeing the smile of a child or patient who recovers safely after a difficult operation. That sums up so much of his philosophy.

- And that's what makes the next step in his life, which the article treats as the peak, so logical—his return to serve his country in an organized and institutional way.

- Which was the founding of the Magdi Yacoub Heart Foundation in Aswan in 2009.

- Yes. And the article explains that this isn't just a hospital—it's a large, comprehensive project. The most important point, and the one that touches people most, is that it provides treatment completely free of charge.

- Completely free of charge—and in this day and age, with such costs, that's something incredible. Especially with its focus on children from all over Egypt, many of whom would have had no other chance for treatment.

- But it's not just treatment, right?

- Of course not. The article explains that it's also a top-level research center and a training hub for doctors and nurses from Egypt and across the region. It's as if he's transplanting his global experience right into the heart of Upper Egypt.

- Exactly. And that gives the whole project another dimension—much deeper than just charity work.

- The article also talks a lot about his personality. His extreme humility is a quality that keeps being mentioned.

- Yes, yes. Despite all the fame and all the achievements, the article shows his unusual insistence that what he does is a duty not a favor.

- That phrase alone says so much: a duty, not a favor.

- Yes—a sense of responsibility toward people and his country, without any feeling of superiority or condescension.

- And maybe that explains why people love him so deeply, and why he's become a true role model for millions of young people—not just doctors.

- A role model for anyone. People see in him the image of the scientist-human, someone who carries people's burdens before anything else.

- So, the article gives us a complete picture of a personality that managed to achieve that difficult balance: global success and fame, and at the same time a very strong connection to his roots and a deep sense of responsibility.

- A true success story—but not just success in reaching the top. Success in using that top position to serve others.

- Exactly.

- And this makes us think about a final point: what is the real meaning of success or achievement? Is it only personal and scientific accomplishments, or is it the impact we leave on people's lives?

- Exactly. The story of Magdi Yacoub, as the article presents it, shows that the human impact carries far more weight. The question then is: how can each of us, in our own place, achieve that same equation—personal ambition and accomplishment on one side, and human commitment on the other?

- A very important question to reflect on. Thank you so much for this deep analysis of the article.

- And thank you.

Omar Sharif

- Welcome to you. Today we're going to look in more detail at an important article we read about the life of a big star we all know: Omar Sharif. The article focuses on the idea that he wasn't just an international actor, and that's it—it describes him as a bridge between East and West.

- Yes, exactly. And that idea of a "bridge" really caught my attention in the article. It's not just a figure of speech—it was a real experience he lived. And the article hints that it wasn't easy—his journey was full of challenges, both personal and artistic.

- Exactly. So today we'll try to understand that story more—see the main stations the article focused on and the legacy he left behind. Let's start from the very beginning, as the article says: Alexandria, and his original name, Michel Shalhoub.

o Yes, and the family also had roots from Syria and Lebanon—that's a detail the article mentions.

o And the artistic beginning was the discovery by Youssef Chahine. That was in what year? Around '54.

o Exactly, in the film 'Struggle in the Valley'—and opposite Faten Hamama. That was a very strong beginning.

o The article points here to a very important detail—he had originally studied mathematics and physics, I mean completely away from that field. Yes, and that part shows how passion can change the path of a person's life. The article connects this to the idea that his heart, I mean, was with art from the start. And that decision surely wasn't easy at that time.

o Of course. And from here the article moves on to his love story with Faten Hamama. That was, as the article says, the talk of the people at the time.

o The talk of the people indeed—a story everyone was following. The article mentions the issue of changing his religion, that he declared Islam so that he could marry her. And together they made a very successful duo in cinema.

o Yes, they made many films together. But the article also says that this relationship later faced difficulties—the busyness of international fame, all the traveling, that had an impact.

o True. The article mentions the point of their separation.

o Yes. But more importantly—and what the article focuses on—is his later statements, where he always said she remained the only love of his life. That gives the relationship a much deeper human dimension.

o Definitely. Now let's move to the really big turning point: Hollywood. The article talks a lot about the film 'Lawrence of Arabia.'

o Lawrence of Arabia, that was in 1962.

o That film, according to the article, gave him enormous fame— international fame that nobody could have imagined like that.

o True. It earned him an Oscar nomination, and he won a Golden Globe too.

o And that opened the door to other big films like 'Doctor Zhivago' and 'Funny Girl.'

- o Here we can say his life completely changed. The article uses exactly that expression to describe this stage—that the West opened its doors wide for him. He wasn't just an Egyptian star anymore—he became a global star known everywhere.

- o But this fame, as the article analyzes, had another side—the inner struggles. The article paints a picture of someone suffering a little under all those lights, with a sense of loneliness, maybe.

- o Mmm. That's what the article hints at: a struggle between being a world-famous star and at the same time feeling a bit of ghurba (being away from one's home), maybe. And also a longing for Egypt, for his roots. And at the same time, his life was shaped abroad. A difficult balance.

- o And the article discusses the idea of identity in depth. Meaning, despite all that international success, he still felt he was a son of the Nile.

- o Exactly. And at the same time, he became a symbol for an entire generation in the Arab world. People saw in him the dream—the dream of international success.

- o And that in itself is a huge responsibility.

- o Of course.

- o In his later years, the article mentions that he began to reduce acting noticeably—maybe looking for more calm.

- o Yes, the article points to that. And it also mentions his diagnosis with Alzheimer's in his final years, and his death in 2015.

- o God have mercy on him. There was a lot of sadness at that time in Egypt and the whole Arab world.

- o In the end, the article concludes that Omar Sharif left behind a long and important history. His legacy was not only the films. The article emphasizes this second role—that he was truly a cultural bridge.

- o That he presented a different image of the East in the West.

- o Exactly. An attractive, respected image, at a time when stereotypes were dominant.

- o So, if we summarize the main ideas of the article: his exceptional journey from the local to the global; his iconic love story with Faten Hamama; the inner struggles he lived through that add depth to his personality; and his most important legacy—that he was a symbol and a bridge between two cultures.

- o That makes us think of one last point, which the article raises implicitly. And that is—

- Beyond the lights and the films, what can we learn from his experience moving between two different worlds?

- Mmm. An important question—how was he able to deal with two different cultures in that way? And how can his story benefit us today, especially in understanding the issue of identity and belonging in our modern world, which has become so interconnected?

- Truly a question worth thinking about.

Safiya Zaghloul

- Welcome everyone. Today we have a very important topic, and through a really engaging article we'll go deeper into the personality of a woman who is truly a landmark in Egypt's history: Safiya Zaghloul. The article we have focuses on something that maybe hasn't gotten enough attention—that she wasn't just the wife of the national leader Saad Zaghloul. No, this is a completely different story. The article presents her as a real leader, with her own voice—a voice for freedom. And of course, the famous title 'Mother of Egyptians.' The article tells us that this wasn't just a label, it had deep meaning for people. So here we'll try to explore the story the article presents and better understand Safiya Zaghloul's impact. We'll also focus a bit on important terms like 'national struggle.'

- Alright, let's start from the very beginning, as the article says. She was born in 1876, the daughter of Mustafa Fahmy Pasha, who was Prime Minister at the time. So we're talking about a distinguished environment. The article describes her as coming from the upper class, and it also mentions her education in foreign schools—details that give us an idea of her cultural background.

- Exactly. And what really stands out in the article is how it shows that, despite her aristocratic upbringing, her personality was strong and cultured. She wasn't isolated from reality at all. Then comes the turning point the article mentions: her marriage to Saad Zaghloul in 1896. And here, the article uses a very precise expression to describe their relationship: a partnership in struggle.

- Wow—partnership in struggle. Those two words alone tell a story. The article explains more—what exactly did that kind of partnership mean?

- Right. The article shows that it wasn't a traditional marriage at all, especially for that time. No, it was really a relationship built on shared ideas and a shared struggle. They were almost one in their national goals. That's why the term partnership in struggle, as the article puts it, is so fitting. It wasn't just her supporting him—this was genuine participation.

- And that brings us to the central point the article discusses at length: the 1919 Revolution. What was her role like, especially during the period when Saad Zaghloul was exiled? What does the article say here?

- Here the article paints a picture of a woman in the heart of the battle. It shows that after Saad was exiled, she didn't retreat at all. On the contrary, she went down herself, organizing women's demonstrations, opening her house for political meetings and national gatherings. That house itself gained a very symbolic name, as the article mentions: the House of the Nation.

- The House of the Nation—wow, that name really carries weight. So what does the article say about why it was called that?

- Of course, the article links that name to the role of the house itself—as a center for the national movement in Saad's absence, a place where people gathered to coordinate positions, a symbol of steadfastness. The article confirms that she was at the front lines—not just hosting, but truly leading in the field.

- I see. And that's what definitely earned her the most famous title: The Mother of Egyptians. The article gives us an interpretation of that title, right?

- Exactly. The article says that this title wasn't just emotional. No, it expressed her role in speaking on behalf of the people and, as the text says, in defending their cause with strength and courage. At that time, people saw in her the comfort and protection of a mother—sacrificing her own comfort for her children and her country. That's why the title stuck and stayed with her. And the article says she continued in that role even after Saad returned, and even after his death.

- There's another very important aspect the article points to—her contribution to women's empowerment. Can we explain a bit more what's meant here, according to the article?

- Sure. The term 'women's empowerment' here is used to refer to Safiya Zaghloul's role in encouraging women to move beyond traditional roles and enter public life. Having a woman like her, strong and in the center of political and national events, as the article describes her, was a huge inspiration for many women at that time. It made them think about participating more—in politics, in education, in social work. It's as if she opened the door. And the article considers that an important part of her impact.

- Really, the picture the article paints of her is very complete—a truly multi-dimensional personality.

- Yes. And even though the article hints that her later years were calmer, after all those events, until her death in 1946, it concludes with a very important point. It emphasizes that her impact still remains, seeing her as a model of the strong, educated, patriotic Egyptian woman. And it uses a beautiful expression at the end: that she set a living example of courage, belonging, and participation.

- So what we understand from reading this article is that Safiya Zaghloul wasn't just a name beside Saad Zaghloul. No, she was truly a central figure in Egypt's national struggle, and an important symbol of women's progress and participation. And that's all very clear from the article itself.

- And here the article can also make us think about a deeper question. If we look at the idea of 'partnership in struggle' that the article highlights between Safiya and Saad, how might that change our view of historical leadership at that time? Could it make us reevaluate the roles of men and women and their complementarity in shaping history? That's a question the article leaves open for reflection.

Taha Hussein

- Welcome! Today we're going to talk about a figure who is a very important landmark in Egypt's literary and intellectual history—Taha Hussein.

- Yes, Taha Hussein.

- We have a nice article that describes him as the Dean of Arabic Literature. And that's not just because of his writings, but because he was the owner of a great enlightenment project.

- Exactly. And the article really makes that clear. It focuses on a central idea—that the mind and will can overcome anything.

- As they say, the power of the mind is stronger than sight.

- Exactly. And Taha Hussein's story is the living example of that. Let's see how the article presents this journey.

- Alright. The beginning was in Upper Egypt in 1889. The article says that when he was about three years old, he lost his sight.

- Yes, because of ophthalmia and medical negligence at that time.

- Exactly. But the amazing thing is, despite these circumstances and being in a big family, he was a very smart and curious child. The article notes that he memorized the entire Qur'an in the kuttab (traditional Qur'an school).

- That point about memorizing the Qur'an—the article considers it essential in shaping him. It wasn't just about his strong memory, but it shaped his Arabic language in a very unique way, which later showed clearly in his style.

- Definitely.

- His journey in education didn't stop there. He went to al-Azhar (University). But the article says that he felt the method of teaching there was a bit traditional.

- Traditional? What do you mean by traditional—you mean the old methods of rote memorization and so on?

- Yes, exactly. It focused more on memorizing and transmitting knowledge rather than encouraging students to think or discuss. There wasn't much support for new thinking.

- I see. And maybe that's what made him look for another place.

- And when the National University—now Cairo University—opened, he found a different space.

- He joined it right away. The article says he was among the first people to enter this university, and there his mind began to open up even more.

- Of course. And the clear evidence was his doctoral thesis on Abu al-'Ala' al-Ma'arri.

- That was very daring at the time. The article considers it proof of his early commitment to the principle of freedom of thought.

- Right. So what does freedom of thought mean? It means that a person can think and express his opinion—even if it's different—without restrictions.

- And his travel to France in 1914 was another major turning point mentioned in the article.

- Very much so. There, not only did he earn a second doctorate, but he also met Madame Suzanne Bresseau, who became his wife and life partner.

- And the article explains how important her role was. She helped him integrate, to adapt and become part of society there.

- She was like his second set of eyes. Her role was absolutely pivotal.

- And when he returned to Egypt, the article focuses on his role in education—as a professor and later as Minister of Education.

- Yes, he was deeply committed to education.

- His vision was very clear—that he had to change the shape of education in Egypt. His famous saying quoted in the article: "Education is like water and air—it is the right of every citizen."

- Exactly. That sums up everything. He was against rote memorization, which is called talqin (learning by rote).

- Talqin means when someone memorizes information without understanding or discussing it.

- Yes. He wanted to move education to a completely different stage—the stage of critical thinking. That's why he encouraged girls' education and the teaching of philosophy.

- All of this came from his belief in rationalism—reliance on reason and logic.

- Exactly. And this was very clear in his books—like 'The Days' of course, and especially 'The Future of Culture in Egypt.'

- That book in particular—the article says how important and daring it was in its time.

- Indeed, because in it he proposed that Egyptian culture is part of the culture of the Mediterranean basin—that it is connected to Europe just as it is to the East.

- And that wasn't just an academic idea at the time—it was a cultural and political vision.

- Of course. And naturally, ideas like this, along with his writings about critiquing heritage and renewing religious discourse, had to face opposition.

- The article uses the word 'fanaticism' to describe that opposition.

- Fanaticism means clinging to one's opinion and rejecting any new or different thought.

- Exactly—blind attachment to one's opinion.

- They attacked him a lot. They accused him of unbelief, and even demanded that his books be banned.

- But what's remarkable, as the article highlights, is that he stood firm in his position.

- Yes, he responded with reason and with the pen. He never backed down. And this shows how strongly he believed in his principles.

- Absolutely.

- And that's what made his influence last until today. We could say that his journey embodies the idea that a word can change a society.

- Yes, indeed.

- His ideas and writings opened discussions and avenues for thought that hadn't existed before. He wasn't just a writer who lost his sight. He was a thinker who saw with his mind much farther ahead—to the future of his country.

- Truly. Reading this article reminds us of many things—the power of will, the importance of real education that depends on understanding and critique rather than memorization.

- And the necessity of defending freedom of thought and constructive criticism.

- Exactly. Even if those ideas shock some people.

- And maybe the question that stays with us after reading this article is: how can we draw inspiration from his experience today—from his determination, rationalism, and courage...

- In order to face our challenges now.

- Yes. How can one word from us contribute to positive change in our society? An important question for us to reflect on.

- Indeed, a question worth thinking about. Thank you so much for this enjoyable discussion.

- Thanks to you.

Omar Khairat

Note: In this podcast, the AI voices occasionally mispronounce the name of Omar Khairat as xērat instead of the correct xáyrat. Please keep in mind that this is an artifact of the AI system and not representative of native pronunciation.

- Today we're going to talk about an artist who's truly an Egyptian icon. His music has this strange power—it tells stories and pulls you into a completely different world without a single word. Of course, we're talking about Omar Khairat.

- Yes, he's definitely an exceptional artist.

- The article we're looking at today tries to solve the puzzle: how does this style touch something so deep in us, expressing part of our Egyptian identity? We want to understand his journey.

- And that really is the point that grabs you—the idea that music alone, instrumental music, can deliver so many emotions and ideas.

- Exactly.

- Sometimes you feel it says what words themselves can't say.

- So, to understand this, maybe we need to go back a bit. The article mentions his upbringing. He was born in 1948 in Sayyida Zaynab, in a house full of art. His grandfather was the composer Mahmoud Khairat.

- Exactly. The environment itself was ready-made. Of course, that helped.

- It's like art ran in his veins, as we say.

- Yes, of course. His academic studies were at the Conservatoire—Western classical music, with all its strict traditions. But what's striking, as the article points out, is that from early on he had the seed of wanting to do something different.

- How so?

- That he wanted to connect what he studied with the spirit of the country, with the Egyptian huwiyya. He wasn't just applying rules and that's it—no, there was a search for a special mix of his own.

- And before he devoted himself completely to composition, there was the stage with Les Petits Chats [a famous Egyptian band].

- Yes, a very important phase.

- That surely introduced him to the public in a different way, bringing him closer to them.

- Exactly. That stage built his artistic personality and his relationship with people. But the real big move that firmly fixed his name in people's memories was his entrance into the world of film and TV scores.

- Yes, soundtracks for movies and series.

- Exactly. That's when his music became part of our lives—woven into the stories we watched and were affected by. It became the voice of our emotions while we watched.

- Alright, let's take that point and look at it more closely. How does his music "speak"? When we hear, for example, "Qadiyyat 'Am Ahmad" or the theme from Damir Abl Hekma, we immediately feel a certain mood.

- Right.

- Sometimes sadness, sometimes hope, sometimes longing. The music of Damir Abl Hekma, in particular, makes me feel a special warmth and strength. How do we explain that? What's the secret recipe?
- Look, this is his genius. The article also hints at this. His blend/mix is truly unique. He doesn't just put a classical phrase next to an Oriental phrase and that's it—no.
- So what then?
- It's like he melts them together. You'll hear the strong classical piano, then suddenly the nay or qanun answers, with a touch of deep, authentic Oriental tarab (emotional musical ecstasy). Or you might find a jazz rhythm slipping in, giving a new kind of vitality.
- Ah, I get it.
- That's his fingerprint. And this blend created a musical language understood by everyone—even by people who wouldn't usually listen to classical or jazz alone. They can understand the story Omar Khairat is telling through melody.
- And maybe that's what explains the great success of other works like al-Khawaga Abdel Qader or al-Liqa al-Thani. Not to mention his bold move into another risky area: making new musical arrangements, reworking the songs of giants like Umm Kulthum and Abdel Halim.
- Exactly. That's a very big risk.
- Of course.
- People know those songs by heart, tied to them in a very strong way. So when he succeeds in presenting them with a new vision that respects the original while adding his own touch, that confirms his artistic power.
- And we see this clearly in his concerts. They're always sold out.
- True. And that's not just a number—it's an indicator of this strong bond.
- Anyone who's attended an Omar Khairat concert says it's an unrepeatable experience. Not just listening to music and that's it.
- Exactly. The atmosphere itself—the deep silence, the focus, the emotion you see on people's faces—that alone is a story. It's like each person is hearing his own tale, his own emotions.
- Yes.
- Here we're talking about the power of art to touch the deepest part of us, going beyond words to reach this shared meaning, this shared feeling. He truly touched people's hearts.

- And he's not just a successful artist—he's become a real source of inspiration for new generations of musicians.

- His role is very important in raising the status of instrumental music in the Arab region, and attracting new audiences who never listened to it before.

- True.

- And despite all these years, he still has the same lasting presence, the same influence. Maybe that's the secret—not just his great art, but also his huge respect for the audience and his humility.

- So, if we wanted to sum it up: Omar Khairat is an example of how music can be a universal language, expressing complex feelings and a cultural identity like the Egyptian huwiyya, without needing a single word.

- And that makes us think of one last point: could instrumental music, like that of Omar Khairat, sometimes be even truer and more accurate in expressing the details inside us? For each of us, what are the stories or emotions that this kind of music stirs inside? That's a question worth thinking about.

lingualism

Visit our website for information on current and upcoming titles and free language learning resources.

www.lingualism.com

www.ingramcontent.com/pod-product-compliance
Lightning Source LLC
Chambersburg PA
CBHW071157120626
46546CB00006B/2300